Towards Discursive Education

As technology continues to advance, the use of computers and the Internet in educational environments has immensely increased. But just how effective has their use been in enhancing children's learning? In this thought-provoking book, Christina E. Erneling conducts a thorough investigation of scholarly journal articles on how computers and the Internet affect learning. She critiques the influential pedagogical theories informing the use of computers in schools – in particular those of Jean Piaget and 'theory of mind' psychology. Erneling introduces and argues for a discursive approach to learning based on the philosophy of Ludwig Wittgenstein and the psychology of Lev Vygotsky. This book not only addresses an urgent pedagogical problem in depth, but also challenges dominant assumptions about learning in both developmental psychology and cognitive science.

CHRISTINA E. ERNELING is Assistant Professor in the Department of Communication Studies at Lund University, Sweden. She is the author of *Understanding Language Acquisition: The Framework of Learning* (1993) and co-editor of two books on cognitive science: *The Mind as a Scientific Object: Between Brain and Culture* (2005) and *The Future of the Cognitive Revolution* (1997).

Towards Discursive Education

Philosophy, Technology, and Modern Education

CHRISTINA E. ERNELING

CAMBRIDGE
UNIVERSITY PRESS

KH

CAMBRIDGE UNIVERSITY PRESS
Cambridge, New York, Melbourne, Madrid, Cape Town, Singapore,
São Paulo, Delhi, Dubai, Tokyo, Mexico City

Cambridge University Press
The Edinburgh Building, Cambridge CB2 8RU, UK

Published in the United States of America by Cambridge University Press,
New York

www.cambridge.org
Information on this title: www.cambridge.org/9780521144025

First published 2010

Printed in the United Kingdom at the University Press, Cambridge

A catalogue record for this publication is available from the British Library

Library of Congress Cataloguing in Publication data
Erneling, Christina E., 1951–
Towards discursive education : philosophy, technology and modern education /
Christina E. Erneling.
p. cm.
Summary: "As technology continues to advance, the use of computers and the
Internet in educational environments has immensely increased. But just how
effective has their use been in enhancing children's learning? In this thought-
provoking book, Christina E. Erneling conducts a thorough investigation of
scholarly journals articles on how computers and the Internet affect learning" –
Provided by publisher.
ISBN 978-0-521-19474-7 (hardback)
1. Education – Effect of technological innovations on. 2. Educational
technology. 3. Internet in education. 4. Critical pedagogy. I. Title.
LB1028.3.E76   2010
370.15′23–dc22

2010005502

ISBN 978-0-521-19474-7 Hardback
ISBN 978-0-521-14402-5 Paperback

10/4/11

For Alf

Contents

Acknowledgements

The idea of studying education technologies and in particular computers was first suggested to me by Åke E. Andersson when he was Director of the Institute for Future Studies in Stockholm, Sweden. I am very grateful for this and for the Institute's financial support during the early phases of this study.

I would also like to thank Rom Harré, Fathali M. Moghaddam, and David R. Olson for reading and commenting on earlier versions of the manuscript, and making many helpful suggestions. It has sometimes been difficult to find books by Piaget and I am grateful to Robert J. Ackermann for making sure I had access to all the books I needed.

The Department of Philosophy at York University, Toronto, Canada has welcomed me as a visiting professor over the years and provided me with an office and other facilities. I am very grateful for this, in particular to Rabia Sallie for her help. I am especially grateful to H. T. Wilson, who has gone through the entire manuscript in detail and made many invaluable comments and suggestions. I would also like to thank my editors at Cambridge University Press.

My husband, Alf Bång, has, as always, been my most important sounding board and critic. Without his intellectual inspiration, challenges, encouragement, and advice I would neither have started nor finished this project.

Needless to say none of the foregoing persons necessarily endorses any of the opinions expressed here, nor are they responsible for any mistakes.

As I have already mentioned, part of this work was financially supported by the Institute of Future Studies, as well as Riksbankens Jublileumsfond, Umeå University, and the Institute of Communication, Lund University, Campus Helsingborg, all in Sweden. This support is gratefully appreciated.

Introduction

In his book *The Mighty Micro. The Impact of the Computer Revolution* (1979) Evans writes

> we have to admit that thousands of years of academic effort all add up to very little understanding of what the teacher is doing when he teaches and how the pupil is learning what he is being taught.
>
> *(Evans, 1979, p. 116)*

Yet Evans goes on to claim that we think education is something simple, something we can easily accomplish if we only find the right formula in science or in technology, or a combination of both. So seductive is this idea of simplicity that Evans himself, in spite of his scepticism, goes on to claim that computers provide a solution to the age-old enigma of education. And he is not alone. Technologies like films, radio, television, Skinner boxes, and computers have all been hailed as the solution to all sorts of educational problems. Backed by the latest in science, the new technology will inspire and motivate pupils, adapt to their individual interests and abilities, give them access to the latest in knowledge, replace teachers, and reform classrooms or even make them obsolete. Schooling will be fun, easy, and successful.

Since the late 1970s these claims and high hopes have been touted for computers and the Internet. The scientific support has primarily come from the ideas of Noam Chomsky and Jean Piaget. Although these thinkers are different in many respects, their shared idea that children, and especially infants, learn language or other things easily and mainly by their own efforts has lent support to computers as ideal learning tools. Computers make learning fun and easy, and require a minimum of intervention from teachers and other adults. This assumption goes hand in hand with a socio-economic rationale. Computer-based education requires less investment and input from parents and teachers. In dual-income families the computer helps with homework when parents do not have the time. Teacher competence seems less in demand, and teachers need only be coaches. Needing fewer teachers and less classroom space is also attractive to school administrators. However, it has become increasingly evident (e.g., Cuban, 2001) that computers have, like all prior technologies, failed to improve schooling radically.

Is it a failure of computers, of their use, or of the science that provides the rationale for their use? I argue that the theories of cognition, cognitive development, and learning informing the use of computers in schools, especially the theories of Jean Piaget, are flawed and partly responsible for the view that computers can and do enhance learning. The problem is thus not so much with the technology itself as with how learning is conceptualised relative to it.

Children and infants are not small proto-scientists testing theories or hypotheses on their own, but social creatures being introduced into social and cultural contexts and norms. The idea of a lone and smiling infant in front of a computer, doing things even his or her parents cannot do, is mistaken. It is mistaken not because infants are unsuccessful learners. Early learning, especially learning one's mother language, is perhaps the most successful learning we know of. But learning one's first language is not primarily a natural process – something one's biological endowment takes care of. It is most importantly a social accomplishment involving not only the infant exercising his or her biological abilities, but other people, a discursive context, and specific, historically situated cultural practices.

Human beings are cultural beings. They become human and acquire human abilities and knowledge not solely as a result of their biological endowment, but as a result of being treated in a special way by other humans. Since prehistoric times humans have changed and cultivated their physical environment – plants, animals, and objects – but also, perhaps most significantly, themselves. Culture is everything which has been changed or modified by humans, and this is especially true of other human beings. To be exiled from one's group is perhaps the most severe punishment that one can suffer. Indeed, being able to participate in social interactions is a precondition for learning other things. This is evident with autistic children, whose inability to engage normally with other humans make them severely handicapped linguistically and cognitively (Greenspan and Shanker, 2004). Greenspan and Shanker, among others, give compelling evidence that the crucial aspect of symbol formation, language, and thinking is not genetic pre-programming (Chomsky) or physical sensori-motor activities (Piaget), but a learned cultural ability. This learning depends on specific types of nurturing and social interactions and other cultural practices. These are passed down and thereby learned by each new generation, dating back to pre-human cultures. It is this crucial aspect of early learning that Piaget, Chomsky, and mainstream psychology have overlooked. The focus on biological aspects has led to simplified models of education. Infant acquisition of symbols, language, and thinking is a paradigm for other learning because of its social nature, not because of its biological dimensions. It is this intense social interaction which makes this learning motivating, enjoyable, and successful. This is the lesson for all learning situations and especially schooling.

There is still much more to learn about how teachers teach and pupils learn – and about what happens in the workshops I call schools. But a good point from which to start our quest is to recognise that it is a joint venture, in which human biology is an enabling condition, but nothing more. Varying and changing social and cultural practices and traditions are the core of learning, and any attempt to escape from this fact, and all the variation and complexity that follows from it, is bound to be futile. Paving the way for a social and discursive approach to learning is my aim.

I The infantilisation of learning

INTRODUCTION: THE PROBLEM SITUATION

Computers and learning

During the last twenty to thirty years, schools have put a monumental amount of money and effort into introducing computer technology.[1] There have been many reasons put forward to justify this, including saving money in the long run, providing education to groups outside traditional schools or to remote regions, preparing pupils for new working conditions, and so on. But one of the main motivations has been the claim that the technology improves the conditions for learning by making education more flexible in its adjustment to the individual, more like real life, more fun, and thus more motivating. It promotes the pupil's own engagement and active involvement in his or her own education. Underlying such beliefs is, I argue, a view that pedagogical thinking has appropriated from developmental cognitive psychology, namely the idea that all learning is like early infant learning, that is, all learning is grounded in biological abilities and is to a large extent innate, automatic, and unconscious. The task of the school is to mimic the conditions of this early learning situation so that learning in schools will improve. Computer technology is not just one resource that is believed capable of doing this, but also one that will succeed where others have failed.

The computer, e-mail, Internet, multimedia, games, and virtual reality technologies are all seen to be bridging the gap between schools and real life (see for example Papert, 1980/1983, 1993; Schank and Cleary, 1995). Furthermore, these technologies are taken to be intrinsically motivating and therefore argued to be recreating the ideal

---

[1] See for example Armstrong and Casement (1998, ch. 1) and the journals listed in the appendix to this book.

situation for learning. And the ideal situation for learning is the one that infants are in: they learn quickly, without explicit instruction, and seem highly motivated. Thus, the theories minimise or even deny the differences between different cognitive skills, as well as the differences in social situation and also the different 'subject matter' of schools and everyday learning – where one is 'natural' and the other is abstract, symbolic, and conventional. Such thinking conceptualises all learning as natural learning in the sense that all learning is based on the individual learners' biological or natural abilities, as contrasted to learning which requires cultural and social interactions of specific kinds. This biological approach has grown stronger in recent years, particularly in the evolutionary approach to cognition and cognitive development (e.g., Bloom, 2004; Buss, 1999, 2005; Hauser, 2000; Hurford, 2007; Pinker, 1984, 1997, 2002, 2007).

Although the idea that school learning in important respects is similar to infant learning is especially prevalent in the literature on computer use in education (see Chapter 2 for a more detailed discussion), it is, I argue, an idea that is more widespread than this. For example, it is found in views which claim that it is essential that learning is fun and enjoyable and that the child is the best judge of both this and what he or she wants to learn. There are increased expectations of immediate satisfaction of subjective needs, and the classroom is turned into a place where an enjoyable experience is more important than learning something new.

The conception of learning underlying this approach to education and educational technology is the topic of this book. I will not discuss, except in passing, the actual use, reception, or effectiveness of computers, including the Internet, but will focus instead on the underlying assumptions about learning, knowledge, and the mind that are utilised in arguments put forth in support of the educational value of computers. The assumptions are to a large extent appropriated uncritically from developmental psychology, and especially from the constructivist approach of Jean Piaget. In particular, I shall focus on his theories in my critical evaluation of what I call the infantilisation of education. Today much of developmental psychology is part of the growing trend towards explaining all psychological traits and behaviours in evolutionary terms. But the evolutionary approach has been part of developmental psychology from the beginning (see Morss, 1990). In Chapter 5 I discuss today's evolutionary psychology, arguing that it is problematic and that Piaget actually recognised and tried (but failed) to solve one crucial challenge to this approach, namely the human being's ability to go beyond the information given.

The infantilisation of learning

Growing up human is a process by which a natural infant is turned into a domesticated creature, a human adult. Important parts of this process include linguistic and cognitive, as well as social, moral, and emotional, development. Much of this process also depends on the infant's natural abilities, some of which he or she shares with many other animals, but it is also crucially dependent on the child's being part of a culture, being engaged in social interactions, and being treated as a human being by others.

When the newly born human infant confronts the environment for the first time, it is a helpless creature that is totally dependent on others to satisfy its needs, orient itself in the environment, and avoid dangers in its surroundings. Although human infants share many abilities with other animals, in many respects the human infant is more helpless than most other newly born creatures. Yet, under normal circumstances,within a few years the infant has acquired its native language, a remarkable ability to deal with its environment, and a complex set of beliefs about both the physical and social world and other people. Unlike its closest relatives among the animals – the primates – humans are biologically adapted for cultural learning (see for example Tomasello, 1999, 2000, 2008; Wexler, 2006).

The helpless infant is transformed into a talking, thinking being, actively involved in and contributing in a modest way to its culture and intellectual heritage, first in the smaller family setting, among its peers, and later in school or similar contexts. This acquisition is a very

impressive achievement, which most children – under normal circumstances – accomplish with ease. It is, however, an ease that seems to be
more difficult for pupils to recapture in later learning situations, especially in formal schools.

For a long time philosophers, educators, and others interested in
learning and the growth of knowledge neglected early infant learning.
Although scholars like John Locke and Jean-Jacques Rousseau were
interested in children, this very early development and learning in
infants were not seen as interesting or important. In contrast, the last
hundred and fifty years have seen a growing interest in this early
cognitive development and learning. The evolutionary biologist
Charles Darwin's study of the language acquisition of his own infant
son (Darwin, 1877/1974), signalled this change, and increasingly over
time infant development has become the central focus of developmental psychology.[2] Although many psychologists have contributed to this
(e.g., Stanley Hall, James Baldwin, Sigmund Freud, Lev Vygotsky), Jean
Piaget and his studies of infants have been crucial (see for example
The Origins of Intelligence in Children, 1936/1963). But Freud's
focus on the first five years as determining much of later behaviour
and personality has perhaps been even more important. Furthermore,
Noam Chomsky's theories of innate language capacity and universal
grammar have since the late 1950s influenced a growing literature on
early infant learning of language.[3] Particularly as a result of Chomsky's
writings, the problem of infant learning has also, and perhaps rather
surprisingly, become a problem in philosophy. A good illustration of
this is Jerry Fodor's generalisations of Chomsky's ideas (Fodor, 1975/
1979). Fodor's conception of an innate language of thought as a pre-
requisite of all learning, especially early conceptual learning, focuses
on the predicament of the infant as a learner.

[2] Most subsequent theories of developmental psychology have been influenced by
evolutionary views and had a strong biological bias, although much of it has been
influenced more by pre-Darwinian than Darwinian ideas (see for example Morss,
1990).

[3] See for example Chomsky (1968, 1975); Pinker (1984, 1997, 2007); and Wanner and
Gleitman (1982).

Instead of being at best a marginal case of learning, infant learning and cognitive development has come to take centre stage and has
become the paradigmatic case of learning (see especially Gopnik,
2009). The idea that later learning – indeed all learning, including
that of the scientist – in crucial aspects is the same as infant learning
has moved even more to the forefront recently. A version of this
idea is found in the work of Gopnik and Meltzoff (1997). They
claim that the cognitive development of children and the growth of
scientific thinking are the same: the infant is a scientist in the crib
(Gopnik, Meltzoff, and Kuhl, 1999).

In pedagogy the same shift in focus can be seen, with infant
learning in this context increasingly taken to be the paradigmatic
case of learning. This focus on the infant is part of what is usually
called the child-centred approach to schooling because it not only
focuses on the child, but also makes the more specific claim that
ideally all learning in school should be like infant learning.[4] An example of the use of this model of learning is, as noted, found in discussions
of the use of computers as learning tools (see for example Papert, 1980/
1993, and the discussion in Chapter 2), but is found in other contexts as
well (Wells, 1999). For example, Seymour Papert (1980/1993) thinks
that all learning can be assimilated into one kind of learning, namely
the one that the infant engages in. He argues that the situation of
learning one's first and native language can be reproduced with the
help of computers. Children learning a simple program language like
LOGO learn maths or other abstract subjects in the same way as a child
learns its first language (for a more detailed discussion, see Chapter 2).
As I show in Chapter 2, many discussions of computers as educational
tools utilise ideas similar to Papert's, and argue that computers support
a learning situation like the infant's and thus enhance this kind of
'natural learning'.[5] Here the central focus is, as noted, the assumptions
about cognition and its development that underlie and inform such

---

[4] However, all child-centred pedagogues do not make this claim.
[5] This ideal of learning underlies many aspect of current pedagogical thinking, stressing
the importance of enjoyable learning situations, where the child sets his or her own

theories of learning. Other aspects of development, though connected with and inseparable from belief change, will not be discussed.

This interest in infant cognitive development and learning in education is especially remarkable since educators traditionally have pointed to the difference between learning in schools and learning in natural settings like the family. In *Democracy and Education* (1916/ 1966, p. 6; see also 1990) John Dewey stresses that there is a difference between the education everybody gets from living with others, and the deliberate education of the young. In the latter type of education the learning of facts and values set up by society is the primary reason for interaction and there is, unlike in other types of learning, little or no learning by sharing activities in immediate and natural settings. Instead, what is learned is stored in symbols, which are often remote from everyday action and personal relationships. It is an artificial, conventional context, which is foreign to everyday life. Emile Durkheim (1922/1956) likewise emphasises that although the unconscious education we get from living with others in society never ceases, it is different from the formal and deliberate schooling of children, which systematically turns them into social beings, in the sense of conforming to the more explicit standards and norms of society. David Hamlyn (1978) also distinguishes between early and later learning, of which the latter typically takes place in schools, stressing that close personal relationships are not the conditions for later learning and that such learning makes use of concepts already acquired. Jerome Bruner (1971) argues that in formal education or schooling, learning occurs outside the context of immediate action and depends on the ability to follow the abstraction of written texts or oral speech. In school, learning is an act in itself, freed from the immediate ends of particular actions, in which the telling and demonstrations involved to help the learner acquire knowledge are taken out of their normal contexts. David Olson (1994), whose primary interest is in the acquisition of reading and writing, likewise stresses the symbolic, conventional, and

goals of learning and also gets immediate satisfaction. The term is used most explicitly by Schank and Cleary (1995), which I discuss in Chapter 2.

out-of-context conditions such skills build upon. The alphabetical script, like other scripts, is a conventional system of notation, and the written text lacks many clues that are present in oral linguistic interactions. For example, the illocutionary force of an utterance – that is, how it should be taken or understood – is less marked in written than in oral face-to-face discourse. Olson (2003) also argues that the school is a bureaucratic institution and as such affords very different conditions for learning from those of more informal settings, like the family. Howard Gardner (1983) distinguishes between education in so-called non-literate societies lacking formal schooling or the equivalent, and that in societies with formal schooling. He stresses the ways in which formal schooling makes use of and develops the different intellectual potentials of individuals. Although these scholars do not present systematic accounts of the difference between the mechanisms involved in the different learning contexts, they all explicitly recognise it.

Many developmental psychologists also make a distinction between early and later cognitive development and learning. Piaget's stage theory of cognitive development – the sensori-motor stage from birth to around two years of age, the stage of concrete operations until six or seven years of age, and then the stage of concrete operations up to the final stage of formal operations around thirteen years of age – is an example of this. Yet Piaget's stress on assimilation and accommodation as the functional processes involved in all cognitive change has, as we will see in Chapters 3 and 4, lent support to the view that all learning is fundamentally like infant learning. Vygotsky's (1934/ 1994, 1978) distinction between elementary and higher mental or psychological functions as a result of acquiring language is another well-known example of a distinction between very early cognitive development and later development. He argues that later, or higher, cognitive development is qualitatively different from earlier, elementary forms: 'Unlike the lower forms, which are characterised by immediacy of intellectual processes, this new activity is mediated by signs' (Vygotsky, 1934/1994, p. 109).

Yet another example, one that I will use in later discussion, is found in the work of David Geary (1995). He makes a distinction between biologically primary and biologically secondary abilities. *Biologically primary abilities* – of which the acquisition of the child's first native language is an example *par excellence* – depend more on biology and less or not at all on social and cultural conditions. *Biologically secondary abilities* build on the earlier acquisition of biologically grounded skills, but depend for their acquisition on specific and varying social and cultural factors. In my subsequent discussion of these differences I will use a slightly different terminology, namely that of *primary and secondary cognitive skills*. My reason for doing this is that, although all human abilities and skills are biological in the sense that they require a body, I want to stress that both sets of skills are cognitive and leave the question of the role of biology versus culture open, at least for now.[6]

Biologically primary cognitive skills, according to Geary (1995), are based on innate, inherently enjoyable abilities, which have an evolutionary origin. They are skills that have evolved in all humans, but also require interaction with normal social and physical surroundings. Examples of such innately based skills shared by all humans are the ability to recognise speech sounds and, after the maturation of the voice box, the ability to produce them (see for example Erneling, 1993 and Chapter 5). Other examples include numerosity, that is, the ability to determine the quantity of a small set of objects and events accurately without counting (see Geary, 1995).

Biologically secondary cognitive skills, on the other hand, co-opt such innate abilities or skills for tasks that are culturally constructed. Such tasks are often taken out of the context of immediate everyday living and interaction, and are symbolic and in many cases highly abstract. Furthermore, they do not seem to be inherently enjoyable for most people (see Geary, 1995). They are much harder to acquire than the early primary skills and are found only in certain societies,

---

[6] I return to a discussion of this in Chapter 6.

where they are taught in special institutions, either in traditional religious schools, in modern secularised schools, or other educational institutions (see for example Gardner, 1983). Later language learning and many later cognitive skills like arithmetic are based on such culturally modified biological skills that have been co-opted. Such culturally variable skills are unrelated to their original (evolved) tasks. For example, the child's innate phonetic ability, which probably evolved in the context of oral language communication, is in literate societies co-opted as an aid in learning to read.[7]

The primary cognitive skills are found in all humans and all cultures, whereas the secondary cognitive skills vary with culture. The acquisition of reading, writing, mathematics, and academic subjects taught in formal education are typical examples of this second type of learning, and are only found in literate societies. The mechanisms underlying the acquisition of the two types of skills differ, for example, in whether or not they are inherently motivating for the child, or whether they require practice and drill to be learned (see Geary, 1995).

In spite of the fact that the main pedagogical tradition distinguishes between learning outside and inside schools, and between primary and secondary cognitive skills or elementary and higher mental functions, many modern educational theories take all learning to be like early and biologically primary learning. They assume that secondary cognitive skills are acquired in more or less the same way as early, biologically primary cognitive skills. As a consequence the task of schools is taken to be the re-creation of the learning conditions that hold for the first type of skills, namely the conditions of infants.[8]

So, on the one hand we seem to have the recognition among some pedagogues and psychologists of important differences between

---

[7] See Geary (1995); Erneling (1993, esp. ch. 7), as well as Chapter 6 in this book.
[8] Another source for seeing computers as a valuable educational tool is no doubt inspired by what has become known as the cognitive revolution in psychology, philosophy, linguistics, and other social and human science, namely the idea that the mind in important aspects functions as a computer program. This is, though, a topic which I will not deal with here. For a discussion of the cognitive revolution see Johnson and Erneling (1997); Erneling and Johnson (2005).

the context of learning in schools and the learning that takes place outside of schools. On the other hand, however, we have arguments for using computers as learning tools on the assumption that all learning, and in particular learning in schools, is like primary cognitive development. This infantilisation of learning is especially prevalent in the discussion of computers as educational technologies, as I show in Chapter 2.

While I do not intend to discuss why this situation has arisen, let me just briefly point to some possibilities. It probably has something to do with the increase in scientific studies of infant development during the last fifty years, which has led to a changed view of infant capabilities. But it is also related to the view of human nature expressed in theories like Piaget's, which have a long history going back at least to Rousseau. It could be related as well to the new situation in information transfer. New technologies like television, and possibly the computer as well, blur the differences between adults and children in a way that societies dominated by the written text as the main source of information transfer did not (Postman, 1996, 1999).

In addition, I think that there is another constant problem in all formal schooling: the challenge to engage and motivate students to learn actively. If all learning could be effortless and enjoyable and not require explicit instruction, much would be gained. But there is a dilemma here: On the one hand, schools provide learning conditions that offer cognitive empowerment independent of natural, untutored experience in concrete contexts. This very disassociation of experience from specific and concrete situations leads to the need for teachers, learning tools, and social institutions to regulate the interaction, and it seems to be less motivating than natural learning situations. On the other hand, these 'artificial' aspects of schools also pose the problem of transferring knowledge from one context to another, that is, from the school to real-life situations. Perhaps it is not surprising that educators, with the more detailed knowledge we now have of early infant development, try to overcome this dilemma by suggesting that we make schools as much like real life as possible. We thereby seek to mimic one of the most successful and enjoyable cases of such learning – infant learning. Infant learning is increasingly seen as the ideal: it is fast, the child seems to be intrinsically motivated, and he or she actively engages in learning without formal teaching or institutional settings, thus overcoming problems of the traditional pedagogical methods and contexts we so far have found in the schools.

As I have indicated, the pedagogical thinkers back such claims by reference to research in developmental psychology. Yet, as we have seen, the relevance of this research is not self-evident. Are there enough similarities between early or primary cognitive development and late or secondary development to justify subsuming all learning and development under the former? To answer this question one has to investigate the assumptions, especially about learning and cognition, that underlie these claims. Therefore it is not enough to look at the pedagogical practices or at the pedagogy used; one has to turn to theories of cognitive development and learning which influence both pedagogy and actual practice.

EDUCATIONAL PRACTICES, PEDAGOGY, AND THEORIES OF LEARNING

Before evaluating a specific scientific theory – in this case what I have called above the concept of 'natural learning' used in modern pedagogical debates – one has to answer the question of what role, if any, scientific theories of learning and cognitive development should play in education. Emile Durkheim (see Durkheim, 1922/1956) makes a useful distinction between education as the actual influence exerted on children by teachers and parents, pedagogy as theories about this practice of education, and the science of education.[9] Educational practices involve social interaction, actions, and social institutions and are sometimes, but not always, based on pedagogical theories, which in their turn are sometimes based on different scientific theories.

---

[9] I am using Durkheim's distinction only to illuminate different levels involved in pedagogical activities. This does not imply that I believe that the rest of Durkheim's ideas are valid.

According to Durkheim, scientists typically seek knowledge for its own sake, without considering practical application. For example, in psychology scientists try to understand and explain the mechanisms and processes involved. Persons engaged in pedagogy reflect on the actual practice of education and try to improve it, and often base these reflections and suggestions for improvements on results from different sciences, including psychology. If we look at the different pedagogues mentioned above and at ideas presented in textbooks, for example in educational psychology (e.g., Berliner and Calfee, 1996), this is the case, and so it is in discussions about the use of computers in schools (see Chapter 2). Although there is relatively little explicit discussion of theories of cognitive development in this context, when it occurs infant learning is taken to be the paradigm for all learning.

Thus, to answer both the fundamental question of how infants are becoming competent adults and the question of how to apply this in education, one needs to turn to a critical discussion of scientific theories of this transformation. Furthermore, it is important to discuss the acquisition of cognitive skills in different contexts and at different stages in development. To improve schools and the learning of crucial cognitive skills, especially in a society that is becoming increasingly dependent on such skills and on new cognitive technologies, it is important to criticise and improve the pedagogical theories underlying practice. This can, in part, be done by critically discussing the theories of learning used.

THE TWO PROBLEMS OF LEARNING AND COGNITIVE
DEVELOPMENT: PRODUCTIVITY AND THE FRAMEWORK

My aim is not to add to the already large collection of facts about how children learn basic cognitive skills to address the specific issue of using computers in schools. The aim is rather to explore the basic assumptions involved in some of the more influential theories used in the debate about computers in schools, and in so doing confront the assumption that all learning is like infant learning. This, however, leads to the further question of what learning, cognitive development, and the acquisition of knowledge involve.

It is important to address these issues because of the fundamental problem that all theories – philosophical, psychological, and pedagogical – have to answer. Such assumptions underlie both the collection and the interpretation of empirical data, because of the 'underdetermination of theory by data'. The Renaissance astronomer Clavius (1538–1612) had already noticed that deductions of the same phenomena could be derived from an infinite number of logically equivalent theories (see for example Harré, 2001). Nelson Goodman (1972) dealt with the same problem in his so-called 'new riddle of induction': how we, from a finite set of experiences of a particular kind, are justified in drawing one conclusion rather than another. For example, he argues, suppose that all emeralds we have observed up to a point t have been green. This would support equally well the generalisations 'All emeralds are green' and 'All emeralds are grue', if 'grue' stands for the property of being green up to point t and blue thereafter. If experience and observations are underdetermined in this way, that is, if infinitely many generalisations can be drawn from observations, interpretation and explanation presuppose hypotheses – in this case about learning and the mind – which limit the generalisations that can be justified as necessary.

Basic assumptions about the mind, thinking and cognition, knowledge and learning guide what one accepts as important to study and limit the interpretation of observations. Since these are the pre-assumptions of the theories used in accounting for learning in schools, they have to be investigated critically in order to assess their pedagogical value. Psychologists and pedagogues often treat as equivalent research and the collection of data, thereby forgetting that research also involves an understanding of which problems the data are supposed to answer. Progress in science is partly a result of empirical studies, but equally important if not more so is the evaluation of the basic assumptions underlying the gathering of data. Advances in our understanding of different phenomena, especially in science, have mainly rested on conceptual reorientation, as the cases of Newton and Darwin demonstrate.

How are we to understand cognitive development, learning, and the acquisition of knowledge? What are the conditions in which individual children and others learn language, master concepts, and acquire knowledge about the world and other human beings? What is the relationship between the learner's innate endowments and abilities, already acquired knowledge, and new experiences? What is the role of experience of the physical and socio-cultural environment? What roles do other human beings and the wider social and cultural context play? These are issues relevant to the initial learning of the infant as well as to the later learning that takes place in formal educational settings. Thus they are relevant for developmental psychologists as well as for pedagogues and educators who want to understand and improve learning in schools. These questions have to be answered in order to evaluate proposals to introduce computers as tools to enable pupils to learn in the way they allegedly learned when they were infants. Is the account of learning which has come to dominate not only developmental psychology, and to some extent philosophy, but also aspects of pedagogical thinking a satisfactory account?

As a starting point for discussion of these more fundamental and conceptual questions I shall focus on the case of the recent debates about and arguments for using computers in schools.[10] These debates expose the fundamental assumptions and ideas involved, and do so in an interesting way, but a discussion of them has to go further into an investigation of theories of cognitive development that are implicitly or explicitly functioning as a basis for pedagogical claims about computers.

The fact that I use computer technology as a case study to get at the underlying assumptions about mental activity and learning which

---

[10] My discussion of these debates is limited to the years between 1990 and 1999, that is, the heyday of the so-called IT-bubble. The literature has since decreased, but the idea of infant learning as an ideal has not. It is still prevalent in many educational debates, as well as in more recent debates about evolutionary psychology.

dominate much pedagogical thinking is not meant to imply that computers, including the use of the Internet, are a negative presence in schools. In order to understand how they function in aid of learning and cognitive development, to evaluate them, and to improve the learning situation, we need to discuss assumptions about learning and cognitive development. By this I mean in particular the assumptions of mainstream, individualistic, universalistic, and mainly biological psychology, which claim both that learning and cognitive development is an individual mental process and that all learning is like infant learning.

The problems of productivity and of the framework

Below I will present what I take to be a basic conceptual dilemma any theory of learning and cognitive development has to resolve. My later discussion and evaluation of the different approaches to learning – the biological-individualistic and the socio-cultural – take their starting point in this conceptual dilemma (for a more detailed discussion of this, see Erneling, 1993).

There are some aspects of cognitive development that are of little interest to learning theorists. For example, neither rote learning or the mindless repetition of what experience provides, nor the change in an organism's cognitive abilities or knowledge due to some purely chemical or physiological change or to maturation (although such changes play a part in learning), has been the focus of theories of learning. Compare, for example, a pupil who has memorised a number of specific multiplications by heart, and is able to repeat them back, but is unable to solve any new examples of multiplications, with a pupil who in addition to the specific examples he or she has been exposed to can go on and solve new ones. The latter is what we refer to as learning because it manifests a change in individual cognitive ability. The latter pupil is able to go beyond the experience and information given, but the former is not. Learning is the result of experience, but not determined by it. Language acquisition is perhaps the best example we have of going beyond the information given in that we are able to produce and understand a potentially infinite set of sentences, but all learning involves the ability to go beyond the information given.

Before going on I also want to distinguish learning and cognitive development from creativity, which, I think, cannot be explained by any theory. If we were in possession of a theory which could explain and predict radical change, the change predicted would already be present in the theory and just making it explicit would not count as creativity (see Erneling, 1993).

So, a theory of learning and cognitive development is not concerned with rote learning, mindless repetition, or creativity, but with going beyond the information given in a structured way. Yet this ability, or skill, builds on the learner's natural abilities and previously acquired skills and knowledge, and thus constitutes, a framework for learning.

The fundamental puzzle any theory of learning and of the growth of knowledge has to confront is how to reconcile the idea of a restrictive framework with the ability to go beyond the information given, and being productive. These two features of learning create a puzzle or dilemma because they pull in different directions.

The problem of productivity

One problem, namely that of productivity, refers to the ability to go beyond information or experience to deal with new situations or contexts, as exemplified in the case of multiplication mentioned above. This ability is, as noted, distinct from creativity, which involves radical conceptual or other change. It is also very clearly exhibited by the language-learning child, by a competent language user, and by anyone who applies what is learned in a specific context to a new situation. This is the case with something as common as the use of words and sentences to describe our experiences. When we describe a specific subjective experience, we must make use of words in a specific combination, but these and the proposition they form must necessarily have a meaning that is more general than the single and specific experience referred to. Describing an object, such as a chair, is not only reporting on a unique perceptual experience, but subsumes something unique under a public and general category. Another example is the case of a pupil learning to subtract who not only is able to repeat all encountered and memorised specific examples of subtraction, but also is able to do subtractions never encountered before. That is, the pupil is able to go beyond experience given and apply it in new situations in a competent way. This is what all educators strive for: a pupil who is moving beyond what the teacher has provided, or even knows or is able to do himself or herself. Gilbert Ryle puts it this way: 'yet the pupil has learned virtually nothing unless he becomes able and ready to do things of his own motion other than what the teacher exported to him' (Ryle, 1967, p. 118).

The problem hinted at here, namely that all our experiences are unique events yet are subsumed under general concepts or general laws or rules, is a special case of going beyond the information given, or the problem of induction. This is the problem of generalising from a finite set of examples to a potentially infinite set. For example, the generalisations 'All crows are black' is typically based on the observation of a large, but finite, set of observations. Yet it is about all instances of crows, even those not observed. In all reasoning or cognitive activity, whether everyday, scientific, or even when using language to communicate, something like induction, or going beyond the information given, is required. Therefore, accounting for the conditions of learning involves one of philosophy's most central and persistent problems. These fundamental assumptions prevalent in philosophy – especially Cartesian–Kantian philosophy – have been adopted by psychology, as will become clear below.

The problem of the framework
The problem of the framework also figures in another of philosophy's perennial problems, namely that of relativism. The relativist claims that mutual understanding between different cultures, different historical times, or different scientific theories is impossible unless one shares a common framework. The same problem arises in learning in

the sense that the teacher and pupil have to share a common framework, and furthermore the individual pupil has to have a framework in order to make sense of and judge what he or she is confronted with in experience. The new experience, which is to be learned, has to fit in with what is already known. In order to benefit from experience, one has to be able to sort out what is relevant from what is not relevant and to connect it with what is already known. Thus, one already has to have an initial framework of knowledge in order to learn something new, though this seems paradoxical. But this problem is not new and was indeed stated by Plato: 'a man cannot search either for what he knows or for what he does not know[.] He cannot search for what he knows – since he knows it, there is no need to search – nor for what he does not know, for he does not know what to look for' (Plato, 1981, 80e). Given this, should we conclude the learning is impossible and that the ability to be creative and to generalise is just an illusion or appearance? While this paradox seems to imply that learning something new is impossible, acquiring something new is at the heart of learning, as described above.

Furthermore, whether or not the pupil has learned something is judged according to an external, public, and normative framework. For example, in the case of learning to multiply, only the answer that fits with the publicly accepted rule of multiplication counts as an instance of learning, not any novel statement. The problem of the framework therefore also has to do with the fact that nothing that is produced is an instance of new knowledge or language use. The new instance of knowledge or language use cannot be a random utterance or action, but has to meet certain criteria.

All theories of learning, cognitive development, and knowledge acquisition have to deal with this problem and in so doing they have to deal *first* with the nature and characteristics of the framework, or more generally with the unlearned givens. To avoid infinite regress there has to be something that is not learned, but, given the paradox mentioned above, this seems to be essentially the same as that which is learned. *Second*, the relationship between what is learned and the framework has to be specified along with the processes or mechanisms involved. *Third,* an account of productivity, or the ability to go beyond the information given, has to be presented.

Different approaches to the mind and to learning answer these questions differently, depending on their 'ideals of psychological order', that is, their conception of the mind, cognition, and cognitive change. Before discussing different psychological approaches to learning, let me begin with a short and very selective presentation of the philosophical underpinning of the learning theories assumed by pedagogical thinking on computers.

THE ACQUISITION OF KNOWLEDGE AS INDIVIDUAL RE-PRESENTATION: THE PHILOSOPHICAL HERITAGE

Historically the problem of learning and cognitive change and the dilemma of productivity and the framework have been part of epistemology, or the theory of knowledge. The two main traditions of rationalism and empiricism provide different ideas on how to resolve the dilemma, yet are fundamentally similar in assuming that learning is a matter of re-presentation. As discussed below, they also share assumptions of universalism and individualism in approaching mental phenomena and cognitive change.

In the rationalist tradition, the acquisition of knowledge is characterised in terms of the inherent or inbuilt (innate) reason and ideas of individual persons, which, although triggered by experience, nevertheless do not change as a result of experience. The claim that new knowledge arises by deduction as a result of new combinations is the account of productivity given by this approach. Experience plays a role, but does not alter the fundamental building blocks of knowledge. Examples of rationalist theories of cognitive growth include Plato's account in the dialogue *Meno,* maturation theories like Arnold Gesell's, Noam Chomsky's theory of the acquisition of grammar, and Fodor's theory of an innate language of thought.

For empiricism, in contrast, learning occurs as a result of the inductive association and re-presentation of impressions given to the mind by experience. Paradigm cases of empiricist theories of learning include John Locke's, David Hume's, and B. F. Skinner's. These theories see the individual learner as passive, an empty vessel into which experiences are poured. A more modern version of this approach is found in evolutionary psychology, with its claim that 'When organisms, including humans, encounter recurrent themes or statistical regularities, natural selection builds such information into their brains, making it an integral part of the survival system' (Hauser, 2000, p. 28).

The framework assumed by these two distinct approaches is different – innate ideas or impressions versus ideas given by experience – but in both, learning and knowledge acquisition are a process of re-presentation of pieces from the basic framework of experience or ideas. Productivity is either a matter of deduction or one of induction. In spite of many differences between them, these two approaches are similar in one fundamental respect, namely the fact that the objectivity and certainty required for claims to count as knowledge are found in the very building blocks of knowledge. In the case of rationalism the building blocks are innate ideas, while for the empiricists they are sense impressions – either encountered by the individual or built in by natural selection, as evolutionary psychologists claim – or in Kant's case, categories of thought. In all cases the building blocks are part of an individual, internal, mental framework.

Since the foundations of knowledge are already present in the form of categories, sense impressions, or ideas, growth is merely a matter of preserving, re-presenting, and combining the already secure foundations. For the rationalists this activity of truth preserving is guaranteed through deduction, while for the empiricist it is achieved through induction, both of which psychologists view as individual internal mental processes. The process of growth could be described as knowledge preserving, rather than being generative of new knowledge. That is, the process of growth in itself adds nothing to what is provided in the fundamental building blocks or framework. The problem to account for in learning and knowledge acquisition, namely that of answering the challenge of the framework as well as that of productivity, is solved in a similar way: by postulating universal and individual, mostly mental representations and processes like innate ideas and sense impressions or mechanisms.

The individual learner is viewed as passive on a fundamental level, someone who is being instructed by the environment either directly, as in the case of sense experiences in traditional empiricism, or indirectly, by innate mechanisms that are the product of natural selection. For rationalists the individual is also passive, in the sense that new knowledge is the result of recombination or of deductions of already inbuilt basic knowledge claims. Learning and the growth of knowledge are in both cases best seen as mechanical or automatic processes, and therefore neither deduction nor induction requires decisions or going beyond the information given (see for example Munz, 2004, p. 16; Fuller, 2003, pp. 199–200).

Another aspect of this mainstream philosophy is to be discovered in the assumptions of individualism, where mainly Cartesian–Kantian assumptions of mental activity are seen to consist of individual and subjective, mostly covert mental processes and their behavioural manifestations. Thinking, remembering, and learning are viewed as individual hidden mental processes, and cognitive change and learning are seen as the result of the interactions of individual 'mechanisms' with the natural and social environment. Knowledge acquisition and conceptual change or learning, in all areas of science as well as in individual cognitive development, are a process internal to the individual, *not* a social achievement. Other people and social institutions are interpreted as aspects of the environment, which in principle have the same type of effects on the learner as the physical environment. The problem of knowledge (and of how knowledge changes) is seen as something that exists for the individual mind in relation to the external world, while other people and social interactions are not supposed to be conditions for knowledge. The growth of knowledge is explained and justified in terms of individual activities like experiences, ideas, hypotheses, and the process of testing and rejecting them. Although all

learners typically interact with other people, this is merely a contingent fact, not one that is essential to the activity. In effect the learner is
like Robinson Crusoe: 'Given resources, longevity, ingenuity and ability, no achievement of science as we know it would, in principle, be
beyond his powers' (Gellner, 1985, p. 107).

These basic shared assumptions of empiricism and rationalism
are found in the most influential psychological accounts of cognitive
development, where traditional learning is taken to be a matter of
individual mechanisms and processes invariant across context. Here
the basic assumptions from philosophy are carried over into aspects of
psychological theories of learning. This is the case for Piaget, who,
although critical of both empiricism and rationalism for failing to see
knowledge growth as a process of construction, shares many of their
assumptions about the mental. Although Piaget has a biological
account of learning and knowledge growth, his theory is sensitive to
the problem of productivity and going beyond the information given.
His thinking can thus be seen, at least in part, as a critique of contemporary evolutionary psychology. This issue is discussed in more
detail in Chapter 5.

TWO 'IDEALS OF PSYCHOLOGICAL ORDER'
Throughout this work I am contrasting two different approaches to
psychological phenomena and especially to learning and cognitive
development: the mainstream approach and, as we shall see later, the
socio-cultural or discursive approach. I argue that so-called natural
learning theories prevalent in the infantilisation of education take
mistaken assumptions about cognitive development and learning
from the mainstream approach, and that the discursive approach provides a better alternative. It is on this fundamental level of basic
assumptions that there are serious problems with the natural learning
theories.

Underlying and guiding my discussion and comparison of the
fundamental assumptions of different approaches to learning and cognitive development is the concept of 'ideals of natural order' (Toulmin,

1961). Stephen Toulmin introduced the concept of 'ideal of natural order' in his 1961 book *Foresight and Understanding: An Enquiry into the Aims of Science*. Toulmin uses 'ideals of natural order' as a conceptual tool to analyse and reconstruct the history of science. He, like Kuhn (1962), wants to replace the traditional view of scientific development as progressive accumulation, with one generation of scientists after another engaging in the same tasks with increasing success. According to Toulmin, the difference between Aristotle and Galileo (Toulmin's major example) is not that Aristotle tries unsuccessfully to do what Galileo later did with success (and Newton after him with even greater success). Instead, Aristotle's view of nature, the questions he asks, and his conception of physical action are different from Galileo's. This difference in ontological assumptions and approach can be summarised as different 'ideals of natural order', which 'mark off for us those happenings in the world around us which do require explanation, by contrasting them with the "natural order of events" – i.e., those that do not' (Toulmin, 1961, p. 79). These fundamental conceptions and assumptions inform the researcher in his or her investigation, and determine which problems are worthy of attention, what counts as an explanation, and even what counts as an empirical fact. According to Toulmin, who develops his ideas with reference to the natural sciences, a given science is at any particular time dominated by one 'ideal of natural order', and once that is replaced it never returns. This limits the applicability of Toulmin's concept. The natural sciences are in several respects different from the social and human sciences, including psychology. More relevant is the point that in psychology one does not find the same historical development as Toulmin thinks typical of the natural sciences. Instead of one dominating 'ideal of natural order' which disappears and is replaced by another, psychology seems to have several competing ideals at one and the same time (although this view has been contested; see for example Palermo, 1971; Gardner, 1985). Gestalt psychology and behaviourism coexisted for a long time, and as Fodor (1980) argues, they represent two different ideals that have coexisted in psychology and that have been present from Descartes to contemporary theories of artificial intelligence. Present-day cognitive science also contains theories with different ideals. For example, biological approaches and computational theories are developing side by side with cultural approaches (see Erneling and Johnson, 2005). This suggests that it may not be appropriate to apply Toulmin's analysis to contemporary psychology. At the very least, however, I think that his approach may be useful for discussing and comparing different theoretical approaches in a particular field in psychology, in this case the psychology of cognitive development and learning. It will help clarify what different approaches to learning and cognitive development take to be relevant problems for explanation, which facts to consider, and how to delimit the subject matter. In this book I show how some very basic assumptions found in mainstream psychology of what learning involves and how it should be explained are mistaken, and I contrast these assumptions with what I take to be a more fruitful 'ideal of psychological order'.

Mainstream psychology's 'ideal of psychological order'
Since the origin of academic psychology in the latter part of the nineteenth century, one approach, which grew out of the philosophical views discussed above, has been dominant. Most psychological theories of learning today treat cognitive development mainly as a matter of changes in individual internal mechanisms, whether neurobiological or psychological, in response to internal changes like maturation and/or interactions with the environment. The framework consists of internal, individual, subjective, mental processes and representations which provide the starting point for cognitive development and the norms of cognitive progression, as well as the mechanism which accounts for productivity or going beyond the information given.

As an example, although Noam Chomsky and Jean Piaget disagree strongly about the innateness of mental structures, especially linguistic or grammatical ones, their fundamental ideas about mental activity and cognition (including linguistic growth) are the same (see Piattelli-Palmarini, 1980). The well-known debate between the two in 1975 focused on this difference, but it is clear from an analysis of this debate that their views of the mental are fundamentally the same.

This is the case because they both accept the same 'ideal of psychological order', that is, the same basic conceptions, assumptions, or paradigms of what mental activity is like, which inform scientists' empirical investigations and explanations. Both are interested in studying cognitive and linguistic growth in order to understand adult cognitive and linguistic activity. Both are interested in universals, in Chomsky's case potential linguistic universals and in Piaget's case the universal of cognition, for example concept of cause. Both also reject empiricist theories of development like behaviourism, and stress the active contribution to learning and development provided by the learner.

Another similarity, which is very relevant when discussing natural learning theories, is that both Piaget and Chomsky think that psychological activity and cognitive change are fundamentally biological and must be explained in those terms. Piaget thinks cognitive growth is based on the same principles as biological development in general. For example, Piaget finds in cognition processes like assimilation, homeorhesis, auto-regulation, and equilibrium, which are also found in all realms of biological activity. For his part, Chomsky stresses that linguistic development is analogous to the development of bodily organs (see also Chomsky, 1997a, 1997b). Both are also psychological realists in the sense that for every psychological activity, perception, learning, thinking or speaking, there is a corresponding bit of individual, private psychological activity. Both see language acquisition as well as cognitive growth as something the individual does or discovers all by himself or herself, with little influence from other people when it comes to the basic structure of cognition or linguistic competence. Piaget argues that cognition arises from individual actions in which the child interacts primarily with the physical environment, with adult teaching and instruction having very little influence on the process of development. According to Chomsky the adult speech the child overhears does not teach or essentially form the basic features of the child's language. The main function of such adult speech is to trigger the developmental process.

Both Chomsky and Piaget account for the framework and pro- ductivity in terms of individual mental processes, which are biologi- cally grounded. In this sense their views are part of the general Western philosophical tradition, according to which problems of knowledge are seen as a matter of whether and how the individual constructs his or her belief system about the world.[11]

This approach interprets human action in a causal mode and sees persons as clusters of mechanisms for processing information, most of which are unconscious. Very often psychological activity is reduced to either biological mechanisms, or mechanical or formal information processing as in modern cognitive science. In spite of persistent prob- lems in accounting for central problems in cognitive development, such as semantics, representation, and subjective experience, this is still the dominant approach, as is evident in evolutionary developmen- tal psychology.

Many of these theories take either animal behaviour (Skinner, 1974) or early infant cognitive activity and learning as their main object of study or paradigm, as in Piaget's studies of his own infant children, or Chomsky's interest in first language learning. The mech- anisms and processes that are presumed to work in the case of animals or infants are assumed to be working in other contexts as well. The conditions for, as well as the mechanisms of, learning are taken to be the same across all species, contexts, and developmental stages, and in this sense are viewed as universal. The idea of universalism, which

[11] Furthermore, the same is true of Jerry Fodor, who generalised and developed Chomsky's views, arguing that first language learning involves an innate language of thought which enables the individual child to form and test hypothesis about the semantic content of language. This argument fails for the same reasons as Piaget's account of cognitive growth fails: it does not account for intentionality and produc- tivity in cognitive change, and assumes in the end the very thing that is to be explained (see Erneling, 1993).

claims that all learning is the same, is also supported by a general tendency towards universalism in psychology, as shown by the tendency to attribute traits like intelligence and aggressiveness across contexts, or the importance given to the pleasure principle in explaining all behaviour (see Kagan, 1998).

Although computational as well as connectionist theories have gained popularity in cognitive science, an important source for the theories under discussion here is biology and especially evolutionary biology. In developmental psychology, mental phenomena like reason and differential cognitive abilities are seen to be no different from other adaptation mechanisms and can be studied in the same way – as biological adaptations to the physical and social world. Nearly all developmental psychologies (such as those of Freud, Piaget, and Skinner) borrowed ideas for psychological mechanisms and developmental 'laws' from Darwinian and especially pre-Darwinian theories.[12] This reinforced a view of the infant as a purely biological being coping with the environment on its own, as well as a tendency to look for accounts of both the framework and productivity in biological processes.

Connected with such generalisations and reinforcing them are other dominant themes in contemporary developmental psychology, like the emphasis on the importance of the first five years for all subsequent development. In effect, the conditions of the child's early social context (e.g., the importance of the parents, especially the mother; see Rich Harris, 1998) and innate biological disposition are taken to form, and even to determine, all future development. The best-known example of this is found in Freud's psychoanalytic theories, but the same idea is also found in behaviourism. Here early environmental factors are thought to have a decisive influence on later development.

In conclusion, this approach views learning and cognitive development primarily as a matter of an individual using the mind to confront and make sense of experience on his or her own. Learning is a structured

---

[12] For a comprehensive discussion of the pre-Darwinian legacy see Morss (1990).

and fundamentally a predetermined process of re-presentation. In critically discussing Piaget's theories as an instance of these assumptions, I hope to show their shortcomings. The two problems of learning – productivity and the framework – can be approached and solved without resorting to the troubling assumptions of individualism, mentalism, biologism, and universalism. This is what the socio-cultural or discursive approach does.

The socio-cultural alternative and its 'ideal of psychological order'

There is a less influential approach, the socio-cultural or discursive one, which sees human life as a collective activity in which linguistic and cognitive developments are the joint enterprises of children and adults. Adults, in close symbiosis with infants, interpret and guide their shared activities in accordance with local rules and norms for skilful cognitive conduct. Children's natural behaviours are interpreted in accordance with folk psychology, and the children are treated accordingly (see Erneling, 1993, and Chapter 6 for a discussion of the role of symbiosis in language acquisition). According to this 'ideal', culture and social interaction are what give order, form, and content to our mental lives, which otherwise would be wild or fluid.

This approach has a history going back to Wilhelm Wundt's *Volkerpsychologie* (1916), Wilhelm Dilthey's *Geisteswissenschaften* (1914–36/1985), the psychology of Lev Vygotsky, and the philosophy of Ludwig Wittgenstein (for a discussion of this see for example Harré, 2000, 2001). This 'ideal of psychological order' has coexisted with more traditional approaches, and is given a greater hearing in recent cognitive psychology (see Erneling 1997, 2007). As an example, cultural psychologists like Bruner (1983, 1990, 1996) and Michael Tomasello (1999, 2008) focus on the fact that children grow up and acquire cognitive skills in the context of a structured social world with games, rituals, and normative and symbolic activities like language, which take place in cultural institutions like families. This rich cultural context is not only a trigger or facilitator for individual cognitive abilities, but constitutes a unique ecological niche, which frames the cognitive activity of the learner while he or she acquires the culturally specific concepts, beliefs, and languages required.

The cultural context of language and other symbolic systems as well as social interactions, together with the child's body and brain, are conceived of as tools, which are used in cognitive activity, both shared and individual. Brain processes and behavioural skills are involved, but mainstream psychology's exclusive focus on the underlying processes and mechanisms as the totality of cognition is rejected. The mainstream approach is criticised for conceiving of mental activity as analogous to a competitive game of tennis, which thereafter is 'explained by reference to the physics of elastic impacts and ballistic trajectories' (see Harré, 2000, p. 4).

Theories developed employing the socio-cultural alternative take the framework for learning to consist of individual natural reactions, behaviours, and neuro-physiological structures as well as the external sociolinguistic and cultural context in which the child/learner is actively engaged. Thus the framework is both individual and external or 'collective'. According to this 'ideal of psychological order', language plays a central constitutive role because linguistic interactions are the main source of the socially formed and differentially transmitted cognitive competencies. An illustration of this is the way Vygotsky's and Wittgenstein's ideas (Wittgenstein, 1953) can be generalised to other kinds of learning as well, and thus provide the basis of the discursive approach to learning. Learning something is a process of domestication or cultivation, of taking something natural and making it into a cultural product. By engaging in different types of cultural discourses, the learner becomes a skilled participant. Here the prototype is the workshop with the master-teacher transferring skills and norms of specific practical or theoretical practices to the apprentice-pupil, enabling some pupils to transcend their teacher's skills, as well as the norms of the practice. Vygotsky's account of cognitive change in terms of the internalisation of public discursive acts provides a better account of what happens when someone learns something (Vygotsky, 1934/1994). His idea of the appropriation of the collective public to become the individual and private, as in the case of social speech turning into egocentric speech and eventually into private thinking, is a more fruitful approach to education than the views of Piaget and contemporary pedagogy. Becoming a skilled participant in different types of discourses is the result of using one's natural skills in close interaction with others. To become an individual is to become culturally integrated, and this is the result of learned participation in varied cultural discourses (see Moghaddam, 2002).

This also rejects the traditional approach to the problem of productivity, which focuses on internal mental mechanisms. Instead it is claimed (and here there is agreement with Piaget's views) that experience is constantly changing and is always new and productive, that is, going beyond the information given. In this view, mental activity is in a fundamental sense productive. This means that the problem of productivity becomes instead one of accounting for what encourages this 'wild' or idiosyncratic activity to conform to certain socially grounded norms or standards.

The socio-cultural or discursive 'ideal of psychological order' differs from the traditional ideal primarily because it does not approach the psychological agent/subject as a solitary consciousness standing against the world, moving from an intrapersonal or private mental world to an interpersonal or social one. But it is also different because it does not accept reductionistic and universalistic assumptions. Reductionism is not accepted because it is too narrow; and because social life varies from cultures to cultures and over time, universalistic assumptions cannot be taken for granted. This 'ideal of psychological order' differs from the more traditional 'ideal' in what kinds of problems it attends to, what counts as an explanation, and what a psychological fact amounts to. By seeing psychological processes like cognitive development or learning as transactional processes, it focuses not on the individual learner but on the learner as part of a social network with others, acting in accordance with institutional and other shared goals and norms. The units of analysis in accounting for cognition and its development are not mental schemas, representations and rules, grammar, or the individual learner's achievements in different 'experimental' situations, but conversational social acts. If concepts like mental rules, representations, or schemas are to have any explanatory value, they are seen to presuppose and be grounded in actual performances and social practices or intersubjective discourses, rather than the other way around. Explanations have to include the individual's innate capabilities and biological constraints and resources, but also the social practices in which the learner is involved.

It is people in a shared form of life that 'create' the psychological sphere for each other. Cognitive development is not a universal, natural, biological process comparable to bodily growth, but a socio-cultural process of interaction and negotiations in which psychological beings are 'designed' or constructed.

In the case of the developing child, it is in these shared, inter-subjective, and discursive practices that the child becomes a cognitive being, which is to say that there are no universal, secure, and certain foundations. In becoming socialised in this way, the child becomes a person with characteristic psychological and cognitive features. And socialisation, contrary to what most traditional psychologies assume, is not a sub-process but the very essence of all development, including cognitive development. There is therefore no distinction between socialisation and cognitive, linguistic, or emotional development. The child is part of the social from the start and cognitive characteristics, language, and belief systems are, given certain biological conditions, the result of social interactions with other people in specific and culturally and historically varied systems. This brings power and politics into psychology. It becomes impossible to study cognitive development and learning without a focus on society, its institutions and interaction patterns as well as its norms and values, since this is where the child develops and becomes a competent cognitive being.

The two approaches just discussed are different not only in how they see human beings – either as a bundle of mechanisms to be explained causally, or as a person involved in joint, rule-guided, normative activities – but also in methodological aspects. The first approach points to natural sciences like physics, chemistry, and especially biology, whereas the latter methodologies are taken from history, anthropology, sociolinguistics, and sociology.

I augment the discussion of both conceptual and methodological differences in Chapters 3 to 6, arguing that the variances are based on fundamentally different 'ideals of psychological orders'. I investigate the view of these two main approaches on cognitive development, and argue that the traditional and dominant accounts are mistaken in two respects. They miss the essential socio-cultural aspect of development and generalise a mistaken view of early infant learning – seen as natural learning – to all learning situations. Instead, in line with the socio-cultural approach, all learning is cultural and social, including infant learning. The 'model' for all learning is the acquisition of secondary cognitive skills, an activity that is social, cultural, and context dependent.

SUMMARY OF THE BOOK

This book is a presentation and discussion of the 'ideal of psychological order' which informs and underlies what I call natural learning theories, and which, polemically stated, has led to an infantilisation and mechanisation of education. The problem of understanding and explaining learning and cognitive development has both an empirical and a conceptual side to it. While there has been a large amount of empirical study of cognitive development and learning, without a clear understanding of what learning involves and of which conceptual and meta-theoretical problems have to be solved, empirical data are difficult to make sense of and employ in order to give a coherent picture of learning. However, resolving meta-theoretical and conceptual issues is only a first step, though a step that is often forgotten. These conceptual issues are my focus. I shall investigate how the two fundamental problems of learning – that of productivity and that of the framework – are resolved in dominant pedagogical views. My focus is on the natural learning theories that are prevalent in many of today's pedagogy and educational reforms, especially in the literature on the educational uses of computer technology.

In this endeavour, I have chosen to focus on arguments for an important educational reform: that of computers as educational tools. As stated above, the fact that I use computer technology as a case study to get at the underlying assumptions about mental activity and learning which dominate pedagogical thinking does not mean that I am against the use of computers in schools. The reason I have chosen this example is rather because I think that it is very important to be able to understand and assess this technology. In order to understand how computer technology in its different forms functions in educational learning, to evaluate it and to improve the learning situation, we need to discuss the pedagogical assumptions involved and how they are grounded in fundamental assumptions of what learning entails. The use of computer technology in schools has had and will have far-reaching consequences. It has already changed, to a considerable extent, the media education is delivered in, by replacing books and direct social interaction with the Internet, e-mail, chat groups, etc. The teacher's role and authority are also changing and new agents, like specialists accessible by e-mail, are being introduced and gaining an ever greater role. Computer technology also provides possibilities for schooling outside the traditional classroom, including especially the pupil's own home. This technology also influences ideals of education, for example by providing us with a view of what counts as information and information processing, namely, what a computer is able to do. In this way it influences the goals of education. Furthermore, educational practices and technologies have intended as well as unintended or collateral effects. The use of Internet and e-mail not only teaches specific skills in locating information with the help of search engines, but also influences the pupil's attitudes to learning in different ways. For example, since the problem solving afforded by computers amplifies calculation and stresses number or quantitative reasoning, creativity, intuition, and feeling are short-changed (see Cuban, 1986). It is thus important to investigate the very assumptions and 'ideals of psychological order' underlying many of the arguments in support of their usefulness.

The literature on educational computer technology seldom explicitly states what assumptions and theories of learning inform the arguments for the educational use of computers.[13] In Chapter 2, on the basis of an extensive and diverse study of the literature, I reconstruct the implicit assumptions and theories of learning. These learning theories in their turn rely on ideas which have been developed in more explicit and sophisticated form by developmental psychologies, for example behaviourism. For a long time behaviourism dominated educational technology, but it has been replaced by theories stressing the learner's own activity and cognitive abilities. The most influential theory responsible for this change is Jean Piaget's genetic epistemology. In addition, he is perhaps the most efficacious theoretician of the child's cognitive development and pedagogy during the last fifty years. He (together with Noam Chomsky) has been influential in the rejection of behaviourism in psychology in general and an important source of the so-called cognitive revolution (see for example Gardner, 1985; Johnson and Erneling, 1997), and is also less directly responsible for the development of evolutionary psychology and more generally the biologisation of psychology itself.

In Chapters 3 and 4 I critically discuss and assess Jean Piaget's answer to the problems of productivity and the framework, which in fundamental respects is informed by the same assumptions as that of the mainstream 'ideal of psychological order', namely individualism, universalism, and naturalism. Although Piaget is a critic of some aspects of the mainstream approach and his constructivism is an improvement on it, he in the end has problems not dissimilar to those of the mainstream approach. To address further the discussion of Piaget's ideas and also basic assumptions of mainstream psychology, in Chapter 5 I discuss what has come to be known as the 'theory theory' of cognitive development (Gopnik and Meltzoff, 1997) as yet another example of the infantilisation of learning and education.

---

[13] See the appendix to this book.

This research, perhaps the fastest growing area in developmental psychology, focuses on children's recognition of other people's thoughts and feelings (see for example *Theory & Psychology*, 14 (5), 2004). The main assumption here is that children develop theories of other people's minds, just as scientists develop theories on the basis of testing hypotheses. In common with Piaget, Chomsky, and psychologists promoting computers in schools, the theory of mind researchers have failed to recognise the fundamental cultural and intersubjective nature of all learning. Infants are motivated to learn not because of their genetic make-up, but because they need and enjoy social interaction. In order to become and stay fully human, social interactions and culture are fundamental. This is a precondition for, rather than the result of, learning. In this context I also briefly discuss evolutionary psychology and its influence on developmental psychology.

In Chapter 6 I present what I think is a more fruitful way of looking at learning and the problems of productivity and the framework, namely the discursive or socio-cultural approach. I illustrate this with an alternative account of first language learning. I have chosen this example because learning language is the example that natural learning theories use in support of their views. By focusing on their most paradigmatic case, I am able to show that by reconceptualising or changing 'ideals of psychological order' along the lines suggested by the socio-cultural or discursive approach, one can solve serious problems presented by the mainstream approach. By using available data on language acquisition, interpreted using a different 'ideal of psychological order', I show that not even the strongest and most paradigmatic case used by natural learning theories is at all like the acquisition of biological primary cognitive skills, but that it is more like the acquisition of secondary skills. If I am correct in this, instead of the infantilisation of all learning, the paradigmatic case should be cultural learning, not natural learning.

In Chapter 7 I trace the mainly negative implications of the mainstream approach for education. I argue that learning and teaching cannot be separated, since learning is inherently a social undertaking which necessarily encompasses the social shaping and construction of skills based on, yet going beyond, natural abilities in accordance with norms of the wider socio-cultural context. Cognitive development and learning are following in the footsteps of others, blazing a new, yet similar trail every time, but also being able to go beyond the trail of others. Cognitive development and learning are about maximising intelligence and rationality, not minimising it by moving back to infancy.

In sum, the book is a discussion of the 'ideal of psychological order' borrowed from mainstream psychology, which informs Piaget's theories and through these the arguments in favour of the pedagogical value of computers in schools. The critique functions as a background for presenting an alternative approach – the domestication model as contrasted with the infantilisation model. Finally I discuss the consequences for pedagogy and education of such a reconceptualisation of what learning and cognitive development involve.

2 Educational technologies and pedagogy

The reasons for introducing computers into schools are, of course, many and varied: There is the social rationale that it is important for every child in a modern society to be able to handle a computer, e-mail, and the Internet. There is the related vocational rationale that schools have to prepare pupils for computerised jobs. There is the IT-industry rationale of building markets of future consumers. There is also the cost–benefit rationale that computers are cheap replacements for expensive teachers, and perhaps even facilitate the closing of costly school buildings. One also finds what one could call the catalyst rationale, that is, that computers are revolutionising society, the school, and even the pupil's cognitive abilities. Finally, and of signal importance, there is the pedagogical rationale of improving learning. The pedagogical discussions start to appear in the 1980s, but it is only during the 1990s that they really increase. This is not surprising, since the technology is still relatively new, expensive, and untried. It is during times of relative controversy that one finds both the justifications and the criticism. Prior to this there is too little of interest to engage scholars. Once the technology has become widespread, it becomes less problematic and less in need of justification. Thus my focus is on the years 1990 to 1999.

This pedagogical rationale and the developmental theories underlying and informing it are, as I stated in Chapter 1, my topic. In this chapter I begin with a short overview of educational technologies used in schools in the last century. While this is followed by a discussion of the pedagogical use of computers,[1] the main topic is the

---

[1] The aim of this chapter is not to discuss and compare different types of computer technologies, but to state the arguments. Thus the general term 'computer technologies' will be used.

pedagogical justifications that have been provided. In the next three chapters I present and assess theories of learning and cognitive development that inform the pedagogical rationale for computer use, especially Piaget's. My focus is, therefore, not on the actual use of computers, their reception, or their effectiveness as educational technologies. To begin with, let me say a few things in general about educational technologies and computers in order to place the subsequent discussion in its broader context.

The actual use of computers in schools has increased rapidly during the last forty years, yet problems of implementation and reception remain. In fact, the obstacles to the use of computers in schools seem in many respects to be of the same kind as those that faced other technologies during the last century (e.g., film, radio, television), that is, a lack of resources, time, access, and expertise (see for example Cuban, 1986; Leggett and Persichitte, 1998).

To get an idea of this it is illustrative to turn to Larry Cuban (1986), who has studied the introduction, reception, and use of films, radio, and television into schools during the twentieth century. He found a common pattern in all cases. In his 1986 book he suggests the possibility that this same pattern will extend to computer use, and his later studies (Cuban, 2001) to a large extent confirm this. First, there are the early assertions, mainly from school boards, superintendents, politicians, manufacturers, and occasionally a teacher, that the new technology will radically change the schools, replace old technology like books, and even change the physical setting to some degree. The new technology is often described as revolutionary, providing students with more direct contact with the world outside the school, and a more enjoyable learning experience, while increasing the motivation to learn, and the prospect of individualised instruction. In the second stage, scientific studies appear, showing the effectiveness of the new technology as equal or superior to that of ones already in use. In the third stage, it becomes evident that the anticipated universal use of the technology has failed. This failure is often blamed on pedagogical conservatism or technological problems, as for example when there are difficulties with computer hardware and software. At this stage studies appear that are more sceptical of the effectiveness of the new technology. Cuban (1986, 2001) shows that typically few teachers use the new technologies and that even if they do, they do not succeed in replacing books or other traditional learning tools. Obviously there are technologies that are now used routinely, but they are usually relatively straightforward tools for learning, like paper and pencil, rather than the ones that transform the learning situation. One example of a straightforward tool for learning is the pocket calculator, which has become very common in the classroom. Already some aspects of computer technologies are used in this way, but this is not the focus of my interest here.

Many of Cuban's case studies of earlier technologies show striking similarities or parallels to what we have heard and read about computers during the last thirty years. For example, Cuban quotes some examples of early enthusiasm concerning technologies. Thomas Edison wrote, with reference to the educational use of film, in 1913: 'Books will be obsolete in the schools', and a few years later 'Scholars will soon be instructed through the eye. It is possible to touch every branch of human knowledge with the motion picture' (quoted in Cuban, 1986, pp. 11, 9). These are claims that are not much different from the ones we have heard in connection with computer technologies. One other technology, the radio, was seen – like the Internet today – as bringing the world and the latest news into the classroom, making the finest teachers available to every child and effectively constituting a 'textbook of the air'. The introduction in the 1950s of television into the schools was, like today's computers, supported by parents, corporations like the Ford Motor Company, and the US government, as well as by politicians like President John F. Kennedy. Educators even viewed the aeroplane in a similar vein. Cuban begins his 1986 book by discussing a photo of a geography lecture taking place in the cabin of an aeroplane in 1927, with the teacher pointing to the earth seen through the windows. This technology, like the others, was seen as affording real-life experience to students, as compared to dull and removed classroom instruction.

But, as mentioned, in spite of enthusiastic endorsement, monetary support, and early positive scientific studies, the actual use of these technologies in classrooms turned out to be modest. Cuban notes that in 1946 films were not used by a third of teachers, and frequent use was restricted to less than a third of teachers. Similar results were found to apply to the use of radio as an instructional medium. A study of television use in 1981 reported that 13 per cent of elementary, 43 per cent of junior-high, and 60 per cent of high school teachers in Maryland used no televisions whatsoever. Explanations for the non-use of technology vary from teachers' lack of skill, costs, inaccessibility of the equipment, and malfunction, to difficulty in fitting the right film, radio, or television programme into the other learning material being presented to students. Some teachers also show a sceptical attitude or even a fear of the new technology. For example, in the 1920s a teacher wrote a poem expressing some concern about the gramophone and radio, not much different from sceptical comments voiced by some teachers about computer use:

Mr. Edison says
That radio will supplant the teacher.
Already one may learn languages by
means of Victrola records.
The moving picture will visualize
what the radio fails to get across.
Teachers will be relegated to the backwoods.
with fire-horses,
And long-haired women;
Or, perhaps shown in museums.
Education will become a matter
of pressing the button.
Perhaps I should get a position at the
switchboard.   *(see Cuban, 1986, p. 5)*

Cuban argues that this sceptical attitude is not surprising, especially given the fact that teachers themselves do not introduce most technology into the classroom. Instead the technology is introduced by people without direct experience of classroom conditions, for example school boards, superintendents, or politicians, who often want to supplement and even to reduce the role of the teacher. For Cuban, effective instruction depends on a complex number of factors in interaction, which the technology promoters seldom address in their obsession with providing simple ways of transmitting knowledge. This is perhaps not surprising, since pragmatic or economic concerns often overshadow concerns about learning.

Although computers have acquired a rather high level of acceptance, similarities to earlier problems with educational technologies remain. In his 2001 book *Oversold and Underused: Computers in the Classroom*, Cuban presents the results of his studies of the use of computer technology in schools and universities in Silicon Valley. He studied the use of computers, and interviewed teachers, students, and others at pre-schools, high schools, and Stanford University. In spite of the fact that he studied an area where computers were introduced early, dominate the area's industry, and are prevalent in the community, the results were similar to what he had reported in his earlier book. For example, few teachers – less than a third – at all levels of education used computers as new ways of teaching in the classroom. Although close to 100 per cent of the professors at Stanford used computers for research, e-mail, and preparing class notes, exams, etc., classroom use was rare. And when they were used, computers did not change the traditional form of classroom teaching. The same was true of the other schools Cuban studied, leading him to conclude that so far computers have failed to change instruction or learning in schools.

Turning to the effectiveness of computers, we once again find problems, or at least reasons to be sceptical about the claims being made. Research into the question of whether educational use of computers improves academic performance has gone on for at least thirty years. Armstrong and Casement (1998),[2] for example, report that the

---

[2] See also Cuban (2001).

evidence from these studies is inconclusive. In some studies there is a slight difference in favour of computer-aided instruction. In others, this kind of instruction is found to benefit only certain groups of students, while sometimes more traditional methods have been reported to be more effective. Overall, computer-aided instruction seems to have been moderately successful, but the evaluation of such results is made more difficult by the poor quality of many of the studies. For example, they often fail to use appropriate control groups. Furthermore, different teachers are used in the test and control groups. Many studies cover only a short period of time (as little as three months in some cases). This makes it difficult to judge long-term effects because of the likely novelty, extra attention, prestige, and other motivating factors which have nothing to do with the computer's long-term educational value. In addition, some studies measure the students' and the teachers' own attitudes towards computer use, which does not necessarily say anything about actual academic achievement.[3] Therefore, we cannot determine whether or to what extent the technology works, and we know even less about why and how it works. More studies are needed, not only about the correlation between computer use and academic achievement, but to find out more about the person using the technology. To evaluate and improve the educational use of computers, we need to know what learning and cognitive growth with this new technology involve. Computer use will undoubtedly continue and increase. The question is whether and to what extent, in addition to being a useful tool like the pocket calculator, it will also enhance learning in specific ways. Although strong claims concerning computers as devices for enhancing learning have been made, little is said about more specific uses.

COMPUTERS AND LEARNING

Much has been said and written – mostly for, but also against – about the educational benefits of different aspects or applications of

---

[3] See Armstrong and Casement (1998) for examples of different kinds of shortcomings. See also Cuban (2001).

computer technology. But surprisingly little has been said about *how* and *why* this technology increases learning, given the amount of time and research and the number of personnel and monetary resources invested in computer technologies in schools.[4] If it is good for education, why precisely do computers enhance learning and for what pedagogical reasons should children be exposed to computers? There is very little discussion of the conditions of learning and few attempts to explain how computers either improve or do not improve learning and cognitive growth. In pedagogical journals aimed at teachers and administrators, much of the discussion has been focused on technological matters and too little on pedagogical matters.[5] In this literature, references to the rather large body of research in developmental psychology are scarce.

In addition, many scientific studies of the effectiveness of computers fail to discuss theories of learning. These studies consist mainly of correlation studies to establish whether or not the technology increases the child's knowledge or skills, and do not discuss how and why computers are effective. Thus, whether these studies report positive correlations, negative correlations, or no correlation, little is found about how and why this technology is better than other tools at enhancing learning.[6]

On the other hand, critics of the educational use of computer technologies are mainly concerned with obstacles to implementation due to economic difficulties and hardware and software problems. Here the major pedagogical reason the technology is questioned is that it fails to help children fully develop their cognitive, sensory, imaginative, and other abilities, and fails to support critical thinking

---

[4] See the appendix for the journals and databases reviewed (1990–9) but not referred to in the text.

[5] See for example Burbules and Callister (2000); Merrill *et al.* (1992).

[6] The general literature in educational psychology addresses issues of learning more explicitly, but seldom addresses the issue of educational computer use; see for example Berliner and Calfee (1996); Bowd, McDougall, and Yewchuck (1997); Hergenhan and Olson (1997); McCown (1999); Rose (1998, 1999).

skills.[7] In common with writers promoting computers, the critics seldom explicitly support their arguments and recommendations with research from learning theory.

Evans, in his book (1979) on the history and future of the computer revolution, claims that in discussions of the educational use of computers, learning is viewed as something unproblematic and simple. The literature on computers in education during the years (1990–9) covered in this study gives a similar impression.[8] In spite of a widespread belief in the pedagogical usefulness of computers, most writers are not concerned with how learning itself is to be accounted for. More specifically, as we shall see later in this chapter, it is assumed that learning takes care of itself because of the innate natural abilities of the learner. This is even more marked in evolutionary psychology, which is discussed in Chapter 5.

For Emile Durkheim, whom we discussed in Chapter 1, most pedagogical discussions take place at the level of practical implementation and the everyday problems of teachers and administrators. Specific problems and the immediate questions of how to get the technology to work, how to fund new acquisitions of machines and software, and how to operate them, etc. dominate pedagogical discussions. When learning is discussed, it is often very generally and sometimes in contradictory terms, and it is often difficult to discern specific ideas about learning, the acquisition of knowledge, and cognitive development. Yet, even if such assumptions are rarely discussed and critically evaluated, implicit ideas about the fundamental nature of learning and cognitive growth inform these texts. The underlying assumptions of learning can in fact be reconstructed and, as I shall show, are very much in line with basic assumptions of the mainstream 'ideal of psychological order' and, more specifically, of Jean Piaget's constructivism.

---

[7] See for example Armstrong and Casement (1998); Postman (1996); Romiszowski (1997); Roszak (1986).

[8] See the appendix.

Early on in the educational use of computers, the most common theory of learning referred to took the form of different versions of behaviourism.[9] During the last thirty years, constructivism – that is, the idea that children actively build their own systems of beliefs – has become the dominant theory of learning and cognitive development. For example, in the *Handbook of Research for Educational Communications and Technology* (Jonassen, 1996) there are several articles dealing with theories of learning used in educational technology research (e.g., behaviourism, cognitivism, constructivism, postmodernism, and critical theory), but it is clear that constructivism has become the dominant account of learning, replacing behaviourism and stressing its own biological underpinnings.[10]

Briefly, constructivist theories claim that beliefs and theories are products of human enquiry and activity rather than given directly from nature through the senses, or from other people. Knowledge is not derived from the environment, but is somehow made – assembled and structured – by each individual. Children are actively constructing and changing their own mental structures, representations, and systems of belief. The best-known and most influential example of constructivism, as already noted, is Jean Piaget's theory of cognitive development, but versions of social constructivism inspired by Lev Vygotsky are also quite common, especially in discussions of the Internet. This is not surprising given the importance, if not total dominance, of Piaget's theories in pedagogy, in developmental psychology, and also to some extent in cognitive psychology. There has been a turning away from transmissions theories, which define learning as the transmission of beliefs, ideas, theories, and skills to the pupil, who passively receives the pre-ordered material. In contrast, today learning is viewed as a process in which the pupils are actively

---

[9] See for example the discussions of Binder (1993); Cook (1993); Schoenfeld (1993); and Vargas (1993); see also Evans (1979).

[10] See for example Armstrong and Casement (1998); Cooper (1993); Crook (1998); De Corte (1990); Hazzan (1999); Jonassen, Carr, and Yueh (1998); Linard (1995); Papert (1980/1993, 1993); Relan and Gillini (1997); Schank and Cleary (1995); Shute and Gawlick-Grendell (1994); Westera (1999); Yarusso (1992).

constructing and creating their own belief systems. In short, internalist theories have replaced externalist ones. This shift is, together with the traditional biological bias of developmental psychology (Morss, 1990), the most important intellectual factor behind the belief that all learning is like infant learning. This is the consequence of the fact that the constructivist focuses on the individual child's natural, innate, biological abilities. These theories see external factors like culture, social interactions, and teachers as enabling, but not as contributing anything important, which puts these views closer to those in the 'camp' of the mainstream 'ideal of psychological order'. The problem is not so much the idea of constructivism itself as how the constructing or learning is accounted for.

COMPUTERS AND LEARNING THEORIES:
THE INFANTILISATION OF LEARNING
Computer technologies are versatile and can be used in education in many and varied ways. They can, for example, be used as tools for drill, as pocket calculators, as typewriters, as spreadsheets, as drawing boards, as translation devices, as libraries, as search tools, as databases, and as books. They also provide films or videos; function as radios, modelling devices, micro-worlds, and simulators; and can host various games, social networks, and virtual reality applications. They can also be used for individual or shared problem solving. The technology combines old ways of representing knowledge with a new medium. For example, hypertext can be viewed as an extension of index use and footnotes, yet affords an immediate interactivity lacking in traditional indexes. The Internet functions partly as a large library, as the yellow pages, as a newsstand, and as a vanity press, but it is also a medium for communication and social interaction. Yet its combination of different media, flexibility, speed, storage space, etc. sets it apart from more traditional ways of using and communicating ideas and information, as do the various ways it opens new channels for communication and social interaction (e.g., Wallace, 1999).

Although the specific pedagogical reasons for supporting these different uses of computers vary, the underlying assumptions about how they promote learning are similar. Advocates of multimedia, for example, stress the way this application supports individualised learning, and Papert (1980/1993) in particular claims that letting children write computer programs supports individualised learning. Most applications are also believed to support the pupil's own activity and to generate learning situations which are more motivating and realistic than traditional school settings. Thus, in spite of the varied uses of computer technology and the relatively little interest in and discussion of how and why computers promote learning, there are some ideas that recur in a variety of writings, both in applied and also in more scholarly journals. Let me provide a summary of these ideas, with a few observations:[11]

1. One of the most prevalent reasons for proposing the educational use of computers is that they are flexible and therefore afford an *individualised* form of instruction that suits the individual child's own natural abilities and preferences. For example, Veenema and Gardner (1996) argue that CD-ROM is a valuable educational tool because its multimedia features not only make a deeper form of understanding within and across disciplines possible, but also open up learning possibilities to a wider spectrum of children. It is especially valuable for those children whose intelligence does not fit the skills usually supported and utilised in the classroom (that is, linguistic, logical-mathematical, and spatial skills). Thus children with musical, kinetic, and other talents get access to learning material in a form more suited to their particular interests and capabilities. Others, like Nelson (1998), argue that the Internet and the World Wide Web provide many different tools, like e-mail, list-servers, chat forums, conferencing, browsers,

---

[11] This summary is based on the articles referred to as well as the literature listed in the appendix. The main bulk of the material is from the years 1990–9. The articles are both from scholarly journals and from journals directed at teachers. I have focused on the latter since they are the ones that have probably had the greatest influence on the promotion and introduction of computers in schools.

search engines, multimedia websites, etc., which appeal to more and different types of intelligence than do traditional instructional tools.

2. A related reason commonly discussed for using computers is that they appeal not only to the intellect, but also to the child's *senses and imagination*, and *make abstract concepts and problems concrete*. For example, Sykes and Reid (1999) describe virtual reality as the ultimate educational technology, because it is fun and exciting – even more fun and exciting than video games – but more importantly because it engages the child's reason as well as its senses in many different ways. Winn and Jackson (1999) argue that virtual reality applications are cheaper, safer, and more accessible than working in real-life settings, and also make abstract concepts like gravity and justice accessible to the senses.

3. In addition, computers are seen as supporting what is called just-in-time learning and situated learning. This refers to the learning of particular skills or gathering of information related to a specific task occurring in a specific context. The medium is seen as flexible in that it facilitates learning which is motivated by specific and *context-dependent* tasks and goals, much like tasks and challenges children encounter outside the classroom (Chiou, 1992; Hudspeth, 1992; McLellan, 1994; Romiszowski, 1997; Winn, 1993).

4. It is furthermore commonly claimed that computers are *fun* to use, provide a *meaningful learning situation*, and help *motivate* children to work (see for example Cooper, 1993). One reason for this is that they provide learning situations (as for example using a CD-ROM) which mimic a real situation very closely. According to Papert, writing programs to build micro-worlds enables the child to control the environment in meaningful and enjoyable ways (Papert, 1980/1993).

5. A related claim is that computers make learning fun by providing *playful* activities like computer games. For example, Robinson (1998) thinks that a most important task in making computers work in educational settings is the design of appropriate computer games that children enjoy. The same idea is found in Kafai's 1995 book *Minds in*

Play: Computer Game Design as a Context for Children's Learning (see also Prensky, 2001).

6. Yet another reason why computers are thought to be effective is that they *get rid of boring and time-consuming activities* like adding and spell checking. This results in more time for enjoyable exploration of things that interest the pupils. Computers are also seen as promoting the learner's critical thinking, mainly by providing *interesting learning situations* and problems that motivate children (see for example Jonassen, Carr, and Yueh, 1998; Papert, 1980/1993; Schank and Cleary 1995).

7. In addition, the technology is seen as promoting *social interaction* between the students themselves, while increasing interactions with teachers and with other people reached through e-mail or the Internet (see for example McGrath, 1998), thereby going outside the narrow school setting.

8. Another recurring theme is that computer technology changes the *relationship between the teacher and the pupils*. In listing twelve different ways in which computer technology changes this relationship, McGrath (1998) focuses specifically on how co-operation and conversation between pupils and teachers increase. Teachers become more like coaches, guides, or facilitators. The technology promotes a 'balance of power' between the teacher and students (McGrath, 1998, p. 59). This is echoed in many articles and books. Even if it is seldom explicitly stated that teachers will disappear, it is clear that the consensus among those who promote computer technology is that it makes students more independent, active, and in charge of their own learning (Papert, 1980/1993). Teachers lose and should lose their role as the 'sage on the stage' (McGrath, 1998), and take on other roles not very clearly defined, such as those of guides and motivators. They are to become more like parents in the sense that they are not a source of knowledge or of structure, but only facilitators, whose main job is to motivate and adjust the learning situation to the individual pupil's requirements (Papert, 1980/1993; Schank and Cleary, 1995). The pupil, assumed to be self-directing and active in his or her own learning, takes

care of learning and cognitive development (see for example, Romiszowski, 1997).

In this context it is interesting to note that critics of educational computer technology like Roszak (1986) and Armstrong and Casement (1998) share the same ideas of what constitutes the ideal learning situation with those who promote computers. But contrary to those referred to above, they claim that computer technology is impeding children's individuality, by overstressing narrow logical thinking at the expense of other mental skills like imagination. Computer technology, they argue, takes learning out of a meaningful context, and motivates and is fun for only a small group of children at best. Computers are not playful but boring, and discourage the ability to think critically. They are bad substitutes for field trips and are not an aid in social interaction with other pupils or with teachers. The critics, as will become clear below, base their judgement on assumptions and theories of learning and development which in important respects are similar to the views they criticise. The disagreement is not about what constitutes a good learning situation and what learning involves, but rather whether or not computers support these.[12]

In sum, in the literature reviewed above (1990–9) it is claimed that computer technology is providing children with opportunities to learn in a situation that is markedly different from traditional classroom settings. The new situation is fun and meaningful; the pupil is on his or her own, actively shaping and choosing from a rich, flexible, and real-life-like set of materials, learning abstract concepts and intellectual skills and facts, as well as developing creativity and imagination in an easy and un-mysterious way. The teacher is standing on the sidelines helping in this process, but not really shaping it. The learner is seen to be actively constructing his or her own beliefs and ideas in a context different from traditional schools. The subject matter of schools is transformed into real-life, concrete problems of the child's

---

[12] See Campbell (1998); Hill (1992); Johnson (1992); Kearsky (1998); and Mayer et al. (1999) for similar discussions.

own choice. Computers bridge the gap between schools and real life. They motivate, with the learning situation closer to infant learning and with teachers more like coaches, or even parents. Underlying these claims is the idea that the ideal learning situation is like that of a young infant learning language or the basics of numbers, or coming to understand other people's psychology. This is explicitly stated in the two books discussed below.

Which, then, are the more general assumptions and theories of learning and cognitive development that underlie these claims? As already mentioned, they all rely on different versions of constructivist theories like Piaget's, but traces of Vygotsky's social constructivism are also found. I think that Chomsky's innatist account of learning is also implicitly present, and has played a role in promoting the belief that teachers are not really needed. Of crucial importance is Chomsky's claim that learning the grammar of one's first language is not aided or shaped in any important respect by the adults surrounding the infant. And since a recurring idea is that learning is a natural activity and is like the learning an infant engages in when he or she is learning a first language, this is not surprising.

Below I present two different examples of books where these assumptions are stated more explicitly, especially the assumption of infant learning as the paradigm of all learning, and then reconstruct their (and other natural learning theory) solutions to the two problems of learning, namely the questions of the framework and of productivity.

COMPUTERS AND THEORIES OF NATURAL LEARNING

The first of my two examples of pedagogical ideas inspired by constructivism that equates all learning to infant learning is from Schank and Cleary's 1995 book *Engines for Education*. In the book the authors argue for a radical change in education with the help of interactive computer-mediated instruction. Such computer-aided education facilitates what they call natural learning as opposed to formal learning, the latter being the form of learning that typically takes place in schools.

Natural learning is typified by the learning that human infants engage in, but is also found in many situations in non-school, everyday settings that children and adults find themselves in. The most important thing about natural learning is that it is intrinsically motivating, and that no instruction or teaching is needed:

> Small children love to learn, at least before they go to school. No 2-year-old has ever taken a walking class, yet any physically healthy 2-year-old can walk. No 3-year-old has taken a talking class, yet every physically healthy 3-year-old can talk. No 4-year-old has taken a course in geography or planning, yet every physically healthy 4-year-old can find a room in his home, knows his neighbourhood, and can navigate around in his own environment ... Children are little learning machines. *(Schank and Cleary, 1995, p. 2)*

The authors go on to claim that parents help children to learn mainly by protecting them from danger and exposing them to new and interesting situations, because children learn by doing things they find intrinsically motivating. It is this situation that the authors want to re-create in schools with the help of computers. Pupils should be free to seek out what they find interesting and motivating, and teachers should act like parents rather than experts, that is, as facilitators and motivators providing interesting situations that suit each individual child.

Natural learning is intrinsically motivating because it is related to the child's own individual interests and ties in with what the child already knows. It is learner driven and involves active participation by the learner, practising skills but also asking questions, and generating and testing answers from experience of particular cases. Schools, according to the authors, do not encourage this, but actively discourage case-based learning as well as natural curiosity and the asking of questions. Instead, traditional schools teach everyone the same material in the same way, and stress the learning of facts rather than skill.

In sum, the authors see natural learning as learner directed because the learner decides both the goal and the means, and provides the answers from his or her own individual experience. The learning is individualised because it starts from the learner's own interests and goals. It is explorative and reflexive because the learner constantly asks questions and modifies the earlier answers or knowledge he or she has already generated. It is like early infant learning mainly because it is inherently motivating and takes the form of learning by doing, that is, learning by practising skills and testing ideas in real situations, beginning with context-specific dependent cases and generalising from them. It also involves what the authors call incidental learning, namely learning something dull while doing something that is fun. Teachers are more like parents and function as motivators and coaches.

To promote natural learning in schools, Schank and Cleary think we need to introduce computer-mediated instruction. This is not because teachers can't do the job required in principle, but because we do not have the time, money, or number of teachers required to emulate natural learning in real-life situations. Therefore we have to turn to computers, which are ideal for this type of learning because of their flexibility, real-life connections, etc.

As I have mentioned above, underlying this view of education and the role of computers therein is a view of human learning which in many respects is inspired by constructivism, especially by Piaget's theory. Although the authors only mention Piaget once, their ideas are in fundamental respects similar to his. Like him, they see learning as an active construction by the individual learner, based on actually doing things or practising skills that in their turn lead to changes in mental structures (scripts, in Schank and Cleary's case). Furthermore, they stress the importance of how something is learned rather than what is learned. As long as something is interesting to the child it is a suitable subject to study. This is similar to Piaget's distinction between learning and development (Piaget, 1964/1993). Like these authors, Piaget is mainly interested in the acquisition of fundamental cognitive skills, and these, he claims, are acquired with any material as long as it engages the child in active construction. This is closely related to the view that the teacher's role is a minor one, since it is what the learner is doing that is important.

Piaget's influence is evident here even if he is not directly referred to. In contrast, Seymour Papert uses Piaget's theories explicitly to support computer-aided learning.[13] Papert has for many years argued systematically for the use of computers to support natural learning of the kind described above. He, perhaps earlier and more than anyone else, defends the educational benefit of computer-based learning technologies.

Originally a mathematician who studied with Jean Piaget for several years, and also one of the best-known researchers at MIT's Media Lab, Papert has had a profound influence on the use of computers as educational tools. Unlike many others, he bases his arguments on a theory of learning which is a modified version of Piaget's ideas of cognitive development. Although Papert criticises Piaget on some matters, he retains Piaget's basic ideas of cognitive development: it is a natural biological process in which the individual child constructs his or her own theories of different subject matters. But Papert rejects Piaget's stage theory, arguing that concrete thinking is involved at all ages of development, not only during the period between two and twelve years, as Piaget assumed. In this sense Papert, more than Piaget, focuses on child learning, especially early learning (see also the discussion in Chapter 5).

Papert invented LOGO, a computer program for elementary schoolchildren. In his book *Mindstorms* (1980/1993) he describes how LOGO gives the child the opportunity to construct simple computer programs. Children construct micro-worlds, that is, simulated worlds, which they then manipulate and learn from. Papert's conception of learning is, as noted, Piagetian. Cognitive development is active construction, adjusting and revising existing mental structures or theories as responses to problems; or, as Papert says, learning by

---

[13] I am concerned with Papert's conception of learning and not with the effectiveness of his proposed educational use of computers; for a discussion of the latter, see for example Armstrong and Casement (1998) and Rozsak (1986).

'debugging'. The most typical example of such natural learning, according to Papert, is learning one's first language in infancy. Indeed, he thinks all learning – including the cognitive activity of scientists – is like this (for a discussion of such claims see Chapter 5). Given the opportunity to work with computers and write programs, children become little scientists or philosophers, utilising their natural infant-like ability to learn. The problem with formal schooling is that it does not support this kind of learning, but computers do:

> it is possible to design computers so that learning to communicate with them can be a natural process, more like learning French by living in France than like trying to learn it through the unnatural process of American foreign-language instruction in classrooms.
>
> *(Papert, 1980/1993, p. 6)*

The metaphor of imitating the way the child learns to talk has been constantly with us in this work.

> *(Papert, 1980/1993, p. 8; see also Papert, 1993)*

Children seem to be innately gifted learners.

> *(Papert, 1980/1993, p. 7; see also pp. 35, 42)*

Thus, all children have an innate, natural ability to learn and are naturally motivated to learn during their first years of life, especially through physical interaction with the environment. In order to illustrate the importance of this early learning further, Papert refers to his own learning experiences prior to two years of age as typical and desirable. At this early age he claims that he learned about gears both through actively handling and playing with different objects and by thinking about them. This learning situation, as well as the context surrounding learning one's first language, can be simulated by giving the child the opportunity to construct simple computer programs in school. The computer is flexible and versatile, simulates many different learning situations, is fun, and 'adjusts' to individual children in ways that traditional school instruction, books, or other learning tools and teachers so far have failed to do. Another strength of the computer is that it makes abstract ideas more concrete and therefore easier to learn. LOGO re-creates the learning situation that children find themselves in before they go to school.

Furthermore, Papert claims, with reference to Piaget, that natural learning does not require teachers in the traditional sense. The role of the teacher in the new computer-dominated schools is that of a motivator and a coach, not a provider of information. Children are actively building their own knowledge on the basis of their innate natural ability to learn, and they learn 'without being taught' (Papert, 1980/1993, p. 7), just as they learn natural language without being taught (Papert, 1980/1993, p. 52).[14]

In his later book *The Children's Machine* (1993), Papert presents similar views on learning, again stressing that LOGO or something like it will improve learning in schools. Learning abstract subjects like mathematics is best achieved by creating situations in which the subject matter is presented in a concrete way, enabling the child to bring his or her natural learning abilities to bear in constructing individual mathematical micro-worlds. Once again Papert refers to infant learning as the model of learning, claiming that schools do not support this kind of learning:

> As an infant she acquired knowledge by exploration. She was in charge of her own learning. Though her parents put knowledge in her path, she chose what she would investigate, determining for herself what she would think about and how she would think about it.
>
> *(Papert, 1993, pp. 9–10)*

> I would agree that learning is a natural act if we are talking about the kind of learning that happens in a healthy relationship between a mother and her baby or between two people getting to know each other. But schooling is not a natural act. Quite the contrary.
>
> *(Papert, 1993, p. 55)*

---

[14] Here, in addition to Piaget's influence, Chomsky's idea of a language acquisition device is evident.

Papert and others discussed above see learning and cognitive development in terms of what I have called primary cognitive abilities, that is, abilities that are innately based, and learned without teaching by all children. These include learning one's first language, learning some basic spatial navigation, learning basic mathematical concepts and counting, and also learning to recognise other people's feelings and intentions. Papert thinks schools infantilise children by not allowing them to be in charge of their own learning, but ironically he and the others infantilise all learners by claiming that learning should be like the learning carried out by infants or very young children. This view of learning infantilises all learners. This is not because it argues that the learner should be in charge of his or her own learning, be motivated, be engaged in tasks that are relevant, and enjoy the experience, all of which are important aspects of successful learning. It does so because all learning is alleged to rest on something very similar to the innate, natural ability of infants to learn language or basic spatial and number skills. Furthermore, all learning is viewed as something the individual engages in on his or her own, independently of the specific social and cultural context.

As mentioned above, this Piaget-inspired view of learning is not restricted to those who support the educational use of computers, but is also found among the sceptics. For example, Armstrong and Casement (1998) argue that learning involves the use of all the senses as well as motor abilities, and endorse the educational approach found in Montessori and Waldorf schools. They do not explicitly refer to Piaget, but their stress on the importance of using the senses and motor skills to construct individually meaningful beliefs is similar to the views found in the two books discussed above, and in much of the literature promoting computers as educational technology. Similar assumptions are found in Rozsak (1986), who argues that computers make use of only a narrow set of cognitive skills, namely logical and procedural thinking. He criticises the educational use of computers for assuming a model of the mind and cognition borrowed from artificial intelligence studies, where the mind and thinking are thought to be similar to the functioning of a computer program. From this he infers that computers support only one kind of thinking, that is, logical deduction or procedural thinking, but fail to help children develop other cognitive abilities like motor abilities, the senses, or imagination.

Thus, both the critics and the advocates of computer technology share many key assumptions about learning, namely that all learning is what is usually referred to as natural learning or the acquisition of cognitively and biologically primary skills. The ideal learning is the learning the infant engages in during his or her early years.

NATURAL LEARNING THEORIES AND THE PROBLEMS OF THE FRAMEWORK AND OF PRODUCTIVITY: A CRITICAL EVALUATION

The literature discussed above addresses many different problems, including the role of the teacher, the motivation of the learner, and individual variations in cognitive capacity, but underlying these more applied pedagogical concerns are fundamental assumptions about what learning involves. In Chapter 1, I said that there are two fundamental problems that any theory of learning has to address: the problem of creativity or productivity and the problem of the framework.

The first, *productivity*, refers to the ability to go beyond the information or experience given to deal with new situations or contexts. The learner has to be able not merely to repeat mindlessly what has been presented, but to apply words, concepts, theories, and skills in new contexts in a way that makes sense and fits with the setting at hand. The problem of *the framework* has to do with the point that not everything claimed to be knowledge actually is knowledge. Knowledge or language cannot just be a random utterance or action, but has to meet certain criteria. It has to fit with experience, and what the individual already knows, and also fit the expectations and norms of correct use in the social context in which it is used. Furthermore, to benefit from experience, the person learning something has to be able to sort out what is relevant from what is not and connect it with what is already known. Thus, one already has to have a framework of knowledge in order to learn something new.

While the views presented above do not explicitly address these questions, several claims or assumptions are relevant when reconstructing their views on productivity and the framework of learning.

One fundamental idea shared by these views is that natural learning has its base in the child's natural or biological, presumably innate, ability to learn. That is, the framework, as well as the processes enabling children and learners in general to go beyond the information given (productivity), is something innate, provided by the child's biological endowments. Just to say that something is natural or innate is not very enlightening, because as biological beings everything humans do has a natural or innate basis. What is interesting is the specific content of the innate framework and the processes by which development takes place. For example, Tomasellso (2000), speaking about early infant development, states that 'The search for the innate aspects of human cognition is scientifically fruitful to the extent, and only to the extent, that it helps us understand the developmental processes at work during human ontogeny, including all the factors that play a role, at what time they play their role, and precisely how they play their role' (Tomasello, 2000, p. 51).

In effect, unless the content of the framework is specified, just claiming that it is innate or natural does not help us understand what is involved in natural learning. For example, is the natural, innate framework similar to Chomsky's or Fodor's innate language module?[15] Is the child born with different specific modules for various areas of cognitive activity as evolutionary psychologists assume, that is, one for grammar, one for numbers, one for spatial relations, and one for other people's psychology?[16] Is the natural framework flexible and open to modification as Skinner assumed?[17] Or is natural ability more as Piaget

---

[15] See for example Chomsky (1975, 1980); Chomsky in Piattelli-Palamarini (1980); and Fodor (1975/1979).

[16] See for example Bloom (2004); Buss (1999, 2005); Fodor (1983).

[17] See Skinner (1974), for example.

suggested, consisting of initial inborn instincts and a law-like pattern of development thorough specific stages?[18] And what role does experience play in the use of this presumed natural and perhaps innate framework? Does experience shape skill or knowledge, as in experience-dependent skills like music, reading, or geography? Or is experience only triggering innate, pre-fixed patterns, as is claimed to be the case with the presumably innate universal grammar or innate theory of mind?[19]

Cognitive development and learning further presuppose that the child can make sense of what he or she is learning. Both the framework and the new information have to be meaningful. The child has to be able to make sense of what he or she encounters. Fodor (1975/1979) thinks this is an argument in favour of an innate language of thought, but as I have shown elsewhere (Erneling, 1993) such a view only raises the problem of how meaningful concepts are acquired and selected in the evolutionary history of humans. Furthermore, using concepts to explore the world and to communicate with others requires one to reapply the concepts as well as use them in the same way as others. To assume that this ability is innate or, as Piaget claims, acquired by individual construction is problematic, as I argue in detail in Chapter 3.

The problem of the framework not only deals with the starting points for learning and experience, but also raises the issue that not everything that is new, that is, an example of going beyond experience, is an instance of learning. Not all speech sounds or grammatical constructions, answers to a mathematical question, or new applications of a word count as an instance of learning something new, unless they conform to the norms or rules of the cognitive activity in question. Cognition is routinely subjected to assessment according to standards set by the cognitive activity in question, such as language, mathematics, or other practices. In this sense all learning is normative. The framework restricts the directions in which one can extend one's experience to cover new cases and situations. This issue is not

---

[18] See Piaget (1964/1968, 1980).

[19] For a discussion of Fodor and Chomsky's views, see Erneling (1993).

explicitly addressed by natural learning theories; rather, once again it is assumed that the child's innate or natural ability of judgement is involved in some way, thereby guaranteeing that the right conclusions or generalisations are drawn from experience. The question here is: what does it mean to say that something natural is setting the standards for what counts as knowledge, correct grammar, or correct arithmetic? An Australian Aboriginal counting sheep, and claiming that he sees many sheep, is as correct according to his culture's norms of counting as the modern Westerner saying he sees ten sheep. Just stating that the ability to count is innate does not help us. This matter is discussed in detail in Chapters 3 and 4, where I discuss Piaget's conception of the framework and of productivity.

The idea that the child's own natural and supposedly innate ability is all that is needed for learning is also evident in the view of the teacher as motivator or coach. Not only are these terms very vague and unspecified, not really telling us anything useful; they also rely on an unspecified and problematic notion of innateness. The fundamental assumption is that the teacher does not contribute anything important to the activity of learning. The learner is like the young child described by Schank and Cleary, that is, the child learning to talk and walk with minimal assistance from others (see Schank and Cleary, 1995, p. 2). Young infants, like the ones Schank and Cleary are describing, seem to be intrinsically motivated to learn language or learn to walk. Experience and social interaction are not believed to be fundamental either to the desire to learn or for the actual content or skill one is learning. Experience like that provided by teachers only triggers learning, but does not shape it or give it meaning. As we see in Chapter 6, even the most paradigmatic case of natural learning – the acquisition of a first language – is dependent on socio-culturally specific experiences and active involvement and shaping by adults.

The processes of learning something and going beyond information – the problem of productivity – are often described as construction or building. Two general accounts of what this construction and building consist of can be found in the literature reviewed above. Papert, for example, describes this process as a process of 'debugging' (see for example Papert, 1980/1993, pp. xiii, 23, and for a concrete example see 60–1), that is, learning from experience by eliminating mistaken views, theories, or hypotheses when they clash with experience. The learner is progressing by testing knowledge claims, theories, or hypotheses, deducing empirical consequences from them, and then comparing them to their own experience. This hypothetical-deductive account is also found in many other writings, including Schank and Cleary's. They also think that learning involves generalisation from specific cases, an inductive mode of learning. By assuming that these activities are natural and innate, these authors presuppose what they are supposed to explain, rather than accounting for the child's cognitive ability. Put another way, the explanation of how such skills are acquired is shifted from ontogeny to phylogeny, as occurred in evolutionary psychology and related approaches to cognitive growth (see Chapter 5).

CONCLUSION

In critically discussing natural learning theories, I do not thereby claim that learning does not require natural endowments, including specifically innate abilities. Nor do I wish to deny that the learning situation has to relate to the child's interest and be relevant to things outside the school. My claim is only that the accounts of natural learning discussed above are not helping us to understand what is involved. One has to dig deeper and investigate the most influential and comprehensive arguments and theories of natural learning that exist. The accounts of natural learning discussed above are, as noted, not primarily aimed at presenting theories of learning, but are concerned with arguing for or against the educational value of computers. They use ideas from developmental psychology and apply them to a set of educational problems. To judge the validity of these theories, we should not stop at the general and quite perfunctory claims just discussed, but turn to the developmental theories themselves and discuss them in order to see whether they are tenable or not. If they fail to account for learning, as I shall argue they do, they also fail to be good guidelines for assessing the pedagogical value of computers in schools, and learning and cognitive growth generally.

This discussion will take us away from pedagogy to some of the most fundamental issues involved in understanding mental activity, namely intention and meaningfulness and the normative nature of mental states and their productivity, that is, going beyond the information given. In my discussion of the assumptions underlying these I have chosen to focus on Piaget, not only because he has clearly influenced the views presented above, but also because his ideas are explicitly stated and argued. This will enable me to evaluate natural learning theories in their most compelling and articulate form. This is important, since if one wishes to evaluate natural learning theories, or any theories, one should assess and criticise them in their strongest form, rather than second hand. Piaget is important because he remains firmly within mainstream psychology, in spite of his effort to go beyond the tradition by, for example, criticising the static view of knowledge growth found in empiricism and rationalism. An evaluation of his basic assumptions is also an evaluation of some aspects of the mainstream 'ideal of psychological order', also found in evolutionary psychology.

3   Piaget and natural learning

Over the last hundred and fifty years public education has become widespread in the Western world. During this time, educators and psychologists have viewed learning mainly as a matter of transmission of culture from teachers to pupils. This conception of learning was expressed most systematically and forcefully in behaviourism, which both underlay and provided the rationale for the early use of educational technologies, including the early use of computers. More recently the constructivist, internalist approach of natural learning theories has replaced this externalist conception of learning.

As we saw in the Chapter 1, it is common to make a distinction between the acquisition of early, so-called primary, biologically grounded, cognitive skills and later learning of the kind that typically takes place in formal schooling. In spite of this, the dominant view among educators as well as developmental psychologists in the internalist tradition is that all learning is natural learning, that is, like the acquisition of biological, primary cognitive skills. Furthermore, cognitive development is compared to biological development in general. Developmental psychologists have always assumed that the biological basis of human learning and cognitive development is central (see for example Morss, 1990), yet in recent years this biological bias has come even further to the fore. The assumption is that cognitive skills are learned in the sense that their acquisition or development requires both interaction with the environment and biologically prepared structures – universal grammar, schemes, instincts, or theories. These structures have a biological basis and are specific to and typical of the human species. They constrain learning by guiding attention and by selecting relevant experiences in order to develop the innate structures. Humans are inherently motivated and biologically 'prepared' to make use of available experiences to acquire language, concepts of causality, movement, number, theories of mind, and even music, morality, and religion, but experience does not shape the fundamental elements or structures of cognition.

This conception of learning is also individualistic in the sense that children are assumed to teach themselves actively some basic concepts and also culturally specific concepts, beliefs, and ideas in the right kind of environment. This is the Robinson Crusoe view of learning: the framework, as well as productivity, of learning is accounted for in terms of individual, inner mental states, which have a biological basis. This view is in line with the mainstream approach to psychological phenomena; it shares its basic conceptual and ontological assumptions on the nature of mental phenomena and cognitive development, and thus has the same 'ideal of psychological order'.

As we have seen, this approach is the prevailing view of learning in the literature on computers as educational technologies. All learning is natural learning, and in important aspects it is just like the kind of learning the infant engages in when he or she is acquiring language, or basic numerosity. Infant learning is the paradigmatic case of learning. As we have seen in the previous chapter, this approach is, both implicitly and explicitly, inspired by the theories of Jean Piaget, who expressed very similar views when writing on educational issues. For example, he claims that the child is able to learn by itself and develop reason and thought 'by achieving them with its own effort and personal experience', and 'by making use of the impulses inherent in childhood itself' (Piaget, 1969/1970, pp. 138, 151). This obviously leads to placing stress on the child's spontaneous activity through 'use of active methods which give broad scope to the spontaneous research of the child and the adolescent' (Piaget, 1948/1973, p. 15).

Furthermore the teacher is not important: 'his role should rather be that of a mentor stimulating initiative and research' (Piaget, 1948/ 1973, p. 16). Learning is the same in all humans, at any age: 'the child obeys the same functional laws as ours' (Piaget, 1969/1970, p. 164).

Thus, Piaget's explicit claims about learning are similar to the ones presented in the previous chapters. However, as I stated above, my focus is not on these claims, but rather on their underlying assumptions.

PIAGET'S ACCOUNT OF PRODUCTIVITY
Stages and processes of cognitive development

Piaget developed one of the most comprehensive theories of cognitive development, encompassing an extensive array of empirical investigations as well as philosophical arguments about the nature of mind, development, and knowledge. His empirical generalisations were based initially on case studies of his own children when they were infants, but later he and his collaborators extended their research to a large number of children of different ages. I do not intend to present or discuss the validity of Piaget's empirical studies or the complex system of theories he developed over the years, but instead wish to focus on his solution to the problems of productivity and the framework. Since his solutions to these problems are to a great extent shared by the natural learning theorists, an evaluation of Piaget is, at least in part, an evaluation of the basic assumptions of such theories.

Piaget sees the development of cognition, which he calls intelligence, as a matter of changes in individual processes, first in physical action and later in internalised mental actions in the form of mental processes that he refers to as operations, structures, and representations. Piaget's most fundamental assumption is that cognitive activity and cognitive development are biological processes, and like all biological processes are forms of biological adaptation to the environment.[1] This fundamentally biological approach to mental activity colours his account of the framework and especially of productivity. It is this biologising of cognitive development that has been emulated by those discussed in Chapter 2 when they assume that all learning,

---

[1] See for example *Biology and Knowledge* (1967/1971) for Piaget's most comprehensive discussion of the fundamental similarities between biological and cognitive processes.

and especially learning in schools, should be like the natural learning of infants. This has led to both the individualisation and the infantilisation of education.

Perhaps the best-known aspect of Piaget's theory of cognitive development is his stage theory. According to this, each child passes through a set of distinctive and qualitatively different stages of cognitive functioning, beginning with the sensori-motor stage, which lasts until approximately the age of two years. It is followed by the preoperational stage, which lasts until around six years of age, and is followed in turn by the stage of concrete operations or thinking. Finally, around the age of twelve children, depending on circumstances, enter the last adult stage of abstract or formal operations. Ages vary, but the stages invariably follow each other in the way stated. Piaget describes the whole process in terms of the active construction of more and more abstract thought structures or schemas and concepts moving towards the objectivity and rationality typical of scientific thinking. Cognitive development thus follows a certain order from the simple to the complex and from the concrete to the abstract, with the earlier stages being serial-sequential prerequisites for the latter.

Cognitive development is the outcome of interactions between an active, changing organism and a constantly changing environment. For cognitive change to take place, Piaget claims, there has to be conflict or incoherence in the mental content, or an imbalance between the action of the organism and the environment (see for example Piaget, 1947/1976). In order to overcome this disequilibrium, the individual constructs new concepts, schemas, or mental structures. 'In short, wherever there is thought, there is the search for coherence' (Piaget, 1950/1965/1995, p. 190). In *Judgement and Reasoning in the Child* he puts it in terms of contradiction of mental content: 'non-contradiction is the state of equilibrium in contrast to the state of permanent disequilibrium which is the normal life of the mind' (Piaget, 1928/1976, p. 170). Piaget sees cognitive development as a structured and self-regulated process, one which is intrinsically motivated in the baby as well as in the schoolchild. It is intrinsically motivated because of the need to overcome incoherence and imbalance (see for example Piaget, 1947/1976, ch. 1). This means that children are not motivated primarily by external rewards like praise and blame, but are – in normal circumstances – motivated by striving to overcome disequilibrium. This process of what Piaget calls equilibration results in the acquisition of more and more structured, complex, and abstract conceptual systems.

Piaget stresses that he is interested in cognitive development and not what he refers to as learning. For him learning is the passive acquisition of facts in the way behaviourist and classical learning theories describe it. Such learning is necessary but not sufficient to explain the fundamental changes in cognition that lead to the growth of knowledge in the individual learner. Social transmission of facts by parents and teachers plays a role, but fundamentally development is a result of the individual acting on his or her own (Piaget, 1964/1993). Active exploration of and acting upon the environment are important for cognitive change, but many different specific experiences lead to the same outcome, and hence experience does not shape the fundamental changes of cognitive structures or the move from one stage to another.

According to Piaget, cognitive development is a natural and, in a fundamental sense, a biological process of adaptation resulting in better and better adaptations as the child reaches later stages. The development is governed by functional invariants of biological change, with the highest stage and ultimate goal or end being adult scientific thinking.

Given Piaget's stage theory, with its stress on the qualitatively different mental structures constructed at the different stages, it would perhaps seem strange that he inspired the view that all learning is like infant learning. Yet this theory has been influential not only because Piaget forcefully argues that infants are intelligent even before they acquire language, but also because cognitive development is governed by the same basic biological laws or principles. The fundamental processes of cognitive development – that is, the assimilation of new material to old structures which change while accommodating new information – are the same at all stages of cognitive development. Since these functional invariants operate on all experience they are prior not in the sense of being innate, but because they constitute conditions for experience (see for example Hamlyn, 1978). That is, every experience involves both assimilation and accommodation, although their relative importance may vary. For example, imitation is mainly assimilation. Thus, in spite of different cognitive structures or schemas at different stages, the functional invariants of the development process are the same across stages and contexts, and thus the same in the infant, toddler, schoolchild, teenager, and scientist. In fact, Piaget claims that these biological functional invariants operate on all levels, from the amoeba to human cognition to social institutions (see Piaget, 1950/1965/1995). The sequence of development is also the same across contexts. In a weak sense, then, Piaget's views are expressing the idea of recapitulation.[2]

To summarise: all learners are intrinsically motivated to construct new structures in order to overcome the imbalance or disequilibrium which is created by new experiences and which changes current mental structures – what Piaget calls the schemas. Cognitive development is an intrinsically motivated individual process of adaptation to new situations. Other people, like parents and teachers, play a minor role as providers of suitable environments, but do not influence motivation or the basic direction of cognitive development or the resulting mental structures. Experience, such as the active manipulation of objects and problem solving, is important for cognitive development. But as long as the child encounters a normal environment with normal opportunities for activity, he or she has the input necessary for cognitive development.

Since Piaget believes that learning processes are uniform across stages and that almost any experience will do, and that infants as well

[2] For a discussion of Piaget's recapitulation ideas, see Morss (1990).

as children are intelligent, intrinsically motivated, and constantly learning, it is not surprising that he inspired the kind of theories discussed in Chapter 2. His biological approach to the central aspects of cognitive development – its productivity, or going beyond the information given, and the mental framework – has been very influential. Piaget and those at the forefront of the educational use of computers conceive of learning as the learner's own intrinsically motivated activity, based on universal biological and innate aptitudes. It is sufficient to discern the universal, individual biological and cognitive mechanisms involved in order to account for the conditions for learning. Given this, and the fact that infant cognitive acquisition in normal circumstances seems to be accomplished easily, enjoyably, and mainly without explicit teaching, the focus on infant learning as an ideal is not surprising.

But it is also problematic, because the ideal rests on assumptions – to a large extent taken from Piaget's theories – which have some serious flaws and fail to account for both productivity and the framework of cognitive development and learning. The focus in the rest of this chapter and the next one is on Piaget's solutions to these problems.

Piaget's account of the productivity of mental activity and cognitive change

All learning and cognitive development involve the ability to go beyond the information or experience given to deal with new situations or contexts. As discussed in Chapter 1, the learner has to be able not merely to repeat mindlessly what has been presented, but to apply words, concepts, theories, and skills in new contexts in a way that makes sense and is appropriate to the context in question. Piaget sees this as one of the central problems that theories of cognitive development have to address, and he claims that traditional theories in both philosophy and psychology have overlooked this fundamental productivity of all mental activity. By having a static view of knowledge these theories, according to Piaget, fail to account for cognitive development, not only in the individual, but in philosophy and in science as well. Cognitive activity is a process of constant construction, and not the manipulation of given and unchanging entities like innate ideas, first principles, or sense experiences.

Piaget refers to himself as a genetic epistemologist, thereby indicating that he has a philosopher's and a biologist's as well as a psychologist's interest in how knowledge changes and grows. In fact, accounting for the emergence of new forms in the natural world – and here he includes the mind and knowledge – is his central concern. Piaget began his career as a biologist: he studied water snails and how they change with changing environments, and his discussion of the relative merits of Lamarckianism and Darwinism, and of the relationship between species and individual organisms, all deal with this problem.[3] Piaget's subsequent interest in epistemology and in cognitive development as a succession of qualitatively different structures, and thus in the emergence of different mental structures in the child, deals with this general problem applied to human learning and development. In an interview he said: 'My real concern is the explanation of what is new in knowledge from one stage of development to the next. How is it possible to attain something new? That's perhaps my central concern' (Bringuier, 1980, p. 19).[4]

In his book *Genetic Epistemology*, Piaget summarises his project in the first paragraph by stating 'Genetic epistemology attempts to explain knowledge, and in particular scientific knowledge, on the basis of its history, its sociogenesis, and especially the psychological origin of the notions and operations upon which it is based' (Piaget, 1970, p. 1).

In *Biology and Knowledge*, Piaget says 'reason itself is not an absolute invariable but is elaborated through a series of creative

---

[3] Chapman (1988) claims that one of the central problems, perhaps the most central and general problem, that concern Piaget is that of universals, or the relationship between parts and the whole. Undeniably, this is a central problem for Piaget, but as already indicated several times above, I think the problem of change and productivity – namely the appearance of new forms or structures in the natural world – is a more fundamental, although not unrelated concern, of his.

[4] See also Piaget in *Le Monde*, 1976, quoted in Rotman (1977, p. 8).

operational constructions' (Piaget, 1967/1971, p. 79). His interest in this problem is, he repeatedly stresses, that of a biologist: 'I was interested in problems of knowledge insofar as they could be approached scientifically, as a biologist would' (Bringuier, 1980, p. 7).

Piaget's studies of the change from infantile instincts to structured action to internalised mental structures, the emergence of objectivity from egocentric and subjective thinking, the emergence of scientific rationality, and his stage theory all deal with this fundamental problem. He was primarily interested not in change, but in how the individual learner goes from a state of having less knowledge to having greater knowledge. Cognition, like all biological structures and processes, moves towards a state of higher adaptability, a more balanced or equilibrated relationship between the organism and the environment. The highest and final stage in cognitive development is reached in scientific reasoning. Piaget claims that his interest is 'the study of the mechanisms of the growth of knowledge ... the passage from states of lesser knowledge to states of more advanced knowledge'. Thus, cognitive development is a normative process in the sense that both the process itself and the end result conform to certain standards or norms.

Change and experience

For Piaget, all mental activity consists of active processes of construction that constantly change the mental structures as well as the interpretations of stimuli. The source of cognition or intelligence is to be discovered in the individual's actions and interactions with the environment. Cognition at any moment is the result of both the environment and certain mental structures or schemas. The child constructs new knowledge by adopting or accommodating existing structures or schemas to the structure of the environment, while assimilating the new experience into the existing structures or schemas. According to this view, all experiences are new in the sense that even the repetitions of a stimulus encountered before are not the same experiences. This is so because they are assimilated into a new mental structure that also changes or accommodates to the stimulus (see Piaget, 1967/1971, p. 4, and 1980, p. 24).

Therefore, for Piaget all mental activity is inherently productive or ceaselessly going beyond the information given, and all experience is novel and assimilated to constantly accommodating mental structures. This fundamental productivity is a result of two general biological processes which govern all organic change: assimilation and accommodation.

In sum, all mental activity is a process of constant change, and what needs to be explained is not so much this constant change as how this leads to increasingly more adaptive stages, which means in the case of cognitive development higher, more objective, certain, and rational forms. The subject matter of genetic epistemology and of Piaget's study of cognitive development and learning is not all possible changes in cognition, but only those that result in greater objectivity, logical consistency, etc. Piaget believes that it is not the task of the genetic psychologist to specify the end result; rather, this is done by the various scientists and by philosophers (see Piaget, 1970, p. 13). He thus borrows his characteristics of the end state from different sciences and philosophies. Given the specified end stages, it is the task of developmental theories to explain the process that ends in these mental structures and contents. It is directed change, not just any change, which is the problem to account for. This is Piaget's central concern: reason, knowledge, objectivity, truth, and logical consistency are not the starting points, but instead the end result of development. In *Psychology and Genetic Epistemology* he says 'In fact, all knowledge is always in a state of development and consists in proceeding from one state to a more complete and efficient one' (Piaget, 1970/1971, p. 6; see also p. 7).

Piaget claims that traditional theories both in psychology and in epistemology are mistaken in that they assume that knowledge is static and the beginning, rather than the end product. Examples of such unchanging foundations of knowledge are Descartes' clear and distinct ideas, Leibniz' monads, Hume's strong and vivid sense impressions, Kant's categories of thought, and Hegel's dialectical concepts (see Piaget 1970/1971). Since contemporary theories of development and learning share such assumptions, this is one of the main reasons why Piaget rejects Chomsky's preformism (see for example Piattelli-Palmarini, 1980) and learning theories (Piaget, 1964/1993), as well as traditional epistemologies like rationalism, empiricism, and, at least in one respect, Kantianism.[5] Piaget's proposed solution turns the traditional assumptions on their heads by assuming that what they take to be the fundamentals of all knowledge are the end result of a constantly changing mental activity. These traditional theories are theories of re-presentation, not theories of going beyond the information given, and are not, according to Piaget, giving an account of the productivity of development and learning.

Let me explain by repeating what I said in Chapter 1: the growth of knowledge has traditionally been the concern of philosophers, with the two main traditions of rationalism and empiricism offering two radically different attempts to account for the possibility of knowledge growth. Kant's transcendental philosophy was an endeavour to overcome some of the problems in these two traditions and to offer a new way out of persistent difficulties. Yet, in spite of fundamental differences between these approaches, in the account of both the starting point and the process of growth, they are similar in one fundamental respect. These traditions assume that objectivity and certainty are found in the very building blocks of knowledge, in innate ideas or first principles, in sense impressions, or in the categories of thought.[6] These fundamental building blocks are assumed to be unchanging and static, a claim which, as we have seen above, Piaget rejects.[7]

---

[5] See especially *Genetic Epistemology* (1970) and *Psychology and Genetic Epistemology* (1970/1971).

[6] See for example Piaget (1970/1971, ch. 1).

[7] Piaget's view is controversial in the sense that many epistemologists have considered psychological data as irrelevant to such inquiries, and based on a misunderstanding of what kind of questions epistemology concerns itself with. According to this view, epistemology's concern is the problem of certain foundations of knowledge, not its growth. Piaget's answer would be that if the certainty and objectivity are an end

Furthermore, since these basic building blocks of knowledge are unchanging, growth is merely a matter of preserving, re-presenting, or combining the already 'epistemologically secure' foundations of innate ideas, categories of thought, or sense impressions. If for the rationalists this process of truth preserving, or new instances of knowledge, is produced and secured through deduction, for the empiricist it is achieved through induction. Thus, the process of growth could be described as knowledge preserving, rather than the generation of new knowledge. Here, the process of growth adds nothing in itself to what is provided in the fundamental building blocks – the innate ideas, sense impressions, and categories of thought. Thus there is no going beyond the information given, and knowledge is thought to be something static or given, according to Piaget. He rejects this, as we have seen, claiming 'knowledge as a process is more than a state' (Piaget, 1970/ 1971, p. 2), and says 'knowledge results from continuous construction, since in each act of understanding, some degree of invention is involved' (Piaget, 1970, p. 77).

For Piaget the aim of a genetic epistemology is expressed in the following statement: 'What we can and should seek is the law of this process [of development]' (Piaget, 1970/1971, p. 3). Furthermore, the necessity of knowledge 'lies at the end and not at the beginning' (Piaget, 1970/1971, p. 3). In this respect Piaget begins to depart from the mainstream 'ideal of psychological order', but, as we shall see, he nevertheless ends up with a view very similar to it.

This rejection of the static starting points or building blocks of traditional epistemology is what Piaget has in mind when he insists that knowledge is a process of continual construction (Piaget, 1970/ 1971, p. 2) and is in perpetual evolution: 'there is never an absolute beginning' (Piaget, 1970/1971, p. 19). Further to this point he claims that knowledge is 'the formation of new structures which did not exist before, either in the external world or in the subject's mind' (Piaget, 1970/1971, p. 77). Earlier on the same page he claims that knowledge

result, any epistemology has to concern itself with development; that is, it is a genetic epistemology.

acquisition is always the result of innovative construction. Knowledge is the end product and not the starting point of cognitive growth.[8]

In *The Development of Thought*, for example, he states that those equilibriums that are fundamental to development are better equilibriums, not just new ones (Piaget, 1977/1978, pp. 3, 4), and that they 'must be the necessary result from psychogenetic constructions, yet conform to a timeless and general standard' (Piaget, 1977/1978, p. 25).

Given these claims, Piaget faces a different task from that of traditional theories of cognitive development. His task becomes the explanation of how rationality, certainty, logical consistency, objectivity, and knowledge are the result of processes of structured development towards an end state, not the absolute beginnings. He has to give an account of the processes by which knowledge grows which is different from the empiricism and rationalism he rejects. This is so because he has to account not for the foundations but for the construction of a process, the end result of which is knowledge. Furthermore, development is not only a process of succession; what comes before it somehow matters for what develops later. This point is expressed in Piaget's view that no stage can be skipped and that their order is invariant.

As we have seen, according to Piaget, the basic processes of dynamic equilibrations come, over time, to result in unchanging and universal standards of rationality and logic. Furthermore, the construction of better and better adaptations follows in a set of stages, and their order is invariant and universal in a way that guarantees the end result. Cognitive development follows a unique and necessary path. Assimilation and accommodation, the processes that utilise and interpret experience, conform to a universal and unchanging framework, which distinguishes this process from mere random change. Piaget in *The Development of Thought* writes that the process has an 'inner necessity' that moves in the direction of more advanced coherence and that previous states 'determine' the states which follow (Piaget, 1977/ 1978, pp. 184, 76). In his debate with Chomsky in 1975 he repeated the

---

[8] See also for example Piaget (1926/1955, pp. 236–7).

same point over and over. For example, he declared 'The hypothesis naturally will be that this increasing necessity arises from auto regulation' (Piaget, 1980, p. 31).

In *Sociological Studies* (1950/1965/1995) he expresses a similar view of the existence of 'a final equilibrium toward which practical and mental coordinations necessarily tend' (Piaget, 1950/1965/1995, p. 82), and later he expresses again this idea that there are 'functional laws of equilibrium such that an individual or collective consciousness can only evolve in a certain direction if it is not to disintegrate' (Piaget, 1950/1965/1995, p. 194).

Development is therefore not the result of random variation, but an orderly progress towards the last stage. Since Piaget rejects both preformism and empiricism, he cannot appeal to innate ideas or experience to account for this progress. For him, although innate capacities like instincts, maturation, and experience all play a role, they do not shape development. But what is shaping or ordering development, then? Where does the necessity Piaget ascribes to development come from? If it emerges from the process of construction, how does he account for it? Is he able to maintain his constructivism (and his rejection of the static views expressed by rationalism and empiricism), yet still account for necessity?

As we have seen, Piaget accounts for change in terms of the two processes of equilibration: assimilation and accommodation. Could they, in addition to providing an account of change, provide the necessary ordering functions? That is, do assimilation and accommodation, as explicated by Piaget, account for the way the child moves from a purely instinctive interaction with the environment towards objectivity, certainty, and a mature set of conceptual structures? How does Piaget explain the normative, even necessary, nature of cognitive development?

I think Piaget is correct in assuming that there is constant change in mental life, and that accounting for productivity is accounting for normative change, not for mere change per se. Any living organism, including humans engaged in cognitive activity, is constantly altered by past events. If events are repeated, they lose their newness and to some extent become habit. Yet any repeated experience of an event is not the same as the original or previous one, since even repetition results in a new experience. All encounters with the environment, including those that involve repeated exposure to a stimulus, correspond to the emergence of novel experiences in the individual. The sum of internal and external conditions in one and the same organism cannot therefore be identical from one situation to the next, even in the case of repetition and habit. Thus, there is no genuine repetition. Change and novelty are intrinsic to any organism, since it possesses a sort of memory that we call its history or development.

But as we have seen, according to Piaget, this process of change is not random or contingent but necessary in both its stages of development and its end result. So the task for Piaget is not to only to account for this intrinsic change, which he does in terms of assimilation and accommodation, but to account for how the necessary order and end state of development come about. Given his rejection of empiricism and rationalism, he cannot refer to innate ideas, which unfold or are triggered by the environment, and the environment is not shaping the development as an empiricist would assume. To account for ordered and goal-directed change towards greater objectivity and certainty – which he takes to be the essential aspect of cognitive development – something more is needed. Piaget's answer is, as we have seen above, that the order is inherent in these functional invariants of equilibrium as the universal laws of development, both in the individual and in science. The invariants are intrinsic features of all organised life and impose inevitability on development.

As we saw in Chapter 2, natural learning theories seem to assume that the child can judge what is interesting, meaningful and relevant to learn, and that teachers have no business imposing external criteria on the child. I think that this view is very much inspired by Piaget's assumptions that I have just discussed. If development follows a necessary path, then schooling becomes a matter of putting the child in a context where this can take shape, and learning becomes fundamentally a simple matter (see Evans, 1979). Children do not need special instruction, just a motivating environment in which they can use their natural abilities.

But are Piaget's claims plausible? There are two main problems with them. The first is that his theory of directed and necessary laws of development and evolution is not supported by biology – that is, by neo-Darwinism. Second, he presupposes what he claims his genetic epistemology explains, namely rationality. There is also a further claim related to his assumption of recapitulation, namely that science, as well as individual cognition, develops according to necessary laws independent of social, cultural, and historical factors (see for example Popper, 1957). Let me explain.

The problem of the productivity of learning involves two problems: accounting for change and accounting for ordered and directed normative change. Traditional epistemological theories assume that the building blocks – Descartes' clear and distinct ideas, Leibniz' monads, Hume's strong and vivid sense impressions, Kant's categories of thought, or Hegel's dialectic, as well as the way these are combined through either induction or deduction – lead to the desired result. Ordered change which leads to knowledge is a re-production of certain foundations in strictly prescribed combinations. Objectivity and certainty are found in the building blocks and in the way they are combined. Piaget rejects this as being a static view which amounts to mere re-production. In its place he proposes the view that there are no static or certain building blocks or foundations, but that mental content – knowledge – is a process. Mental representations are constantly changing (this is something he takes as characteristic of all life) by constant assimilation of new material and accommodation of the existing mental schemas and structures. But this is not mere random change, but change that is necessary. The problem, then, for Piaget is to explain this necessity, both in the order of change (stages) and in the end result, that is, 'from less to more sufficient knowledge' (Piaget, 1970, p. 12). Piaget sometimes refers to the functional invariants of assimilation and accommodation and at other times to equilibration, to homeostasis, and to reflective abstraction (see for example, Piaget, 1967/1971).

Problems with Piaget's account

There are several problems with using the processes of assimilation and accommodation to account for cognitive development, that is, progress towards a necessary end state – rationality, objectivity, etc. – as Piaget conceives of it. First, Piaget claims all changes in biological organisms are the result of these processes, and 'cognitive functions, just like any other function, have to observe the common law of assimilation and accommodation' (Piaget, 1967/1971, p. 33). Having said this, however, only certain instances of change, namely those of the human mind, lead to the development of logic, objectivity, and rationality. There has to be something special about assimilation and accommodation, but what? Piaget is aware of the problem. His answer – that the cognitive systems are more differentiated than other systems – does not solve the problem, because one still has to ask what is special about this differentiation as compared to other, non-cognitive cases. One possible answer is that the mind, unlike for example the stomach, is an intelligent or rational system for processing information. This, however, is ruled out because rationality is the end product of the developmental process, and not its starting point. Yet this is what Piaget seems to be suggesting when he claims that in the sole case of the mind development is rational.

Second, the claim that cognitive change is the result of equilibrations – that is, of recognising and reconciling conflict or inconsistency – implies that the individual possesses standards by which to judge imbalance or conflict, as well as inconsistency between propositions describing mental content at a later age. Thus, in the case of cognition, standards of non-conflict, balance, rationality, truth, logic, and objectivity have to be present. But these are, Piaget claims, the end result of the developmental change, not that which is prior in the sense of ordering experience. Continuous assimilation and accommodation lead to these standards, but do not presuppose them. To answer this,

Piaget has to show how standards which are not normatively rational lead to rational standards. More generally, he has to show how weaker structures and concepts lead to stronger ones.

Fodor (1975/1979) has criticised Piaget for being unable to explain development in assuming that cognitive development or learning can be decomposed into stages, where the concepts expressed in the earlier stages are weaker than and different from the concepts in the later stages. Again, the problem is that Piaget has to account for how to go from weaker concepts or schemas to stronger or higher ones. This fails, Fodor argues, because Piaget has to assume what he takes to be the final product as the starting point. Fodor's argument is that in order to learn a new concept one already has to have a conceptual system which is as rich as the one that one is learning. One cannot learn that P falls under R unless one has a language in which P and R are already represented. That is, one cannot learn, for example, that a table is a piece of furniture with four legs and a flat surface unless one already has the concept of flat surface, legs, four, table, and furniture. This Fodor takes to be a strong defence of preformism in learning. He argues that Piaget's description of the transition from one stage to the next in terms of changing equilibriums, by which is meant the correspondence between conceptual schema and the world, does not tell us anything about how the change is accomplished, or what learning is. It only characterises the end result. Thus, according to Fodor, Piaget does not have a theory of learning or cognitive development.

Could there be some other process guiding assimilation and accommodation towards increasingly abstract and objective schemas? In *Biology and Knowledge* (1967/1971), Piaget refers to 'reflective abstraction'. This guides assimilation and accommodation, making the transitions from lower to higher levels of development possible (see also Piattelli-Palmarini, 1980, pp. 66ff.). The problem with this concept, according to Macnamara (1976), is that it could be replaced by 'rationality', which puts us back to square one by ascribing rationality and intelligence to the developing system when, according to Piaget, this is the result, not the starting point.

Hamlyn (1978) makes a similar point in discussing Piaget's reference to homeorhesis, namely that Piaget seems to lack an account of learning, development, and productivity of cognitive development. Piaget's reference to cognitive development in terms of Waddington's concept of homeorhesis, which characterises an organism and which functions to restore not a static but a dynamic equilibrium, moves progressively from one equilibrium towards another higher form of equilibrium. Again, it seems that the orderly principle of progressive rationality is built into the system, thereby assuming precisely what Piaget wants to explain. The concept of homeorhesis only says that developmental or evolutionary processes maintain a directive, progressive trajectory. Piaget thinks that his accounts of cognitive development, comparative psychology, and the history of scientific ideas support this idea. But as Hamlyn (1978) and others argue, to describe something as necessarily progressive is not to give an account of the mechanism, laws, etc. involved. 'As far as Piaget is concerned, and for the present purposes, the important question that now arises is *how* the later stages emerge out of the earlier ones' (Hamlyn, 1978, p. 49).

Messerly (1996) argues that Piaget assumes what needs to be shown, namely that later stages are a necessary progression from earlier ones. First, Messerly points out that Piaget assumes, without argument, that adult knowledge is the reference point from which to judge the child's progression. Even though the claim that adults know more than children is rather uncontroversial, to claim that adults think in a different and better way is not as self-evident. And Piaget gives us no specific argument for this assumption. Furthermore, Messerly argues, Piaget's claim that reason must evolve rationally (see for example Piaget, 1980) is problematic because it assumes that our cognitive faculties are reliable and that there is cognitive progress. While Piaget may have shown 'that there is a connection between reason evolving rationally and cognitive reliability and progress, it does not show that cognitive faculties evolved this way' (Messerly, 1996, p. 135). To refer to the functional invariants of development as progressive does not resolve the matter, and referring to adaptation only begs the question by transferring it from individual cognitive development to biological laws of development.

Piaget, I think, falls back on a few basic assumptions which guide all of his work, namely that the process of cognitive development is both unique and necessary because determined by evolutionary laws. Given what we know about biological and evolutionary change, there is no reason to assume a unique, goal-directed path of development in evolution or in the individual. Neo-Darwinism strongly emphasises that evolutionary direction is contingent and only progressive in particular and limited circumstances. Natural selection works on changes that occur by chance, but this selection is unplanned, and unpredictable except in limited circumstances. Of course survival is progress, but it is a by-product of selection, which contains no plan or mechanism for a specific chain of progressive changes as assumed by Piaget. So falling back on evolutionary laws governing all aspects of life is not a solution. It locates the problem elsewhere, in evolution, and in an account of evolution that is itself problematic.

Piaget sometimes claims that he is not interested in the individual as an individual, but in the epistemological subject, namely that which is common to all.

There is the 'psychological subject', centred in the conscious ego whose functional role is incontestable but which is not the origin of any structure of general knowledge; but there is also the 'epistemic subject' or that which is common to all subjects at the same level of development, whose cognitive structures derive from the most general mechanisms for the coordination of actions.

(Piaget and Beth, 1961/1966, p. 308)

One reason for this is that development can only be inevitable if in its essential aspects it is not influenced by contingent social, cultural, and historical circumstances which influence particular individuals. In this sense the individual is passive in the capacity to influence development, since knowledge grows according to biological laws. Piaget eliminates the learner's role and replaces it with the workings of the cognitive system, and it is this system which responds to disequilibrium by assimilation and accommodation. The way the subject attributes meaning or significance seems irrelevant. Thus Piaget seems to reduce knowledge to biological processes, or at the very least is obliged to close the gap between biology and meaningful cognition (see for example Rotman, 1977, pp. 85, 100–1).[9] His references to recapitulation, which assume that the laws of all developmental change are the same, do not solve the problem but are part and parcel of it. According to this view, the history of humankind and individual cognitive development are evolutionary systems in which all (inherent) possibilities are destined to come into being by unfolding over time. This unfolding or development is in a specific direction, towards a higher, more perfect end state, and is subject to a law of progress. The direction of change is not only necessary, but takes the form of an ordered sequence of stages. The same general laws are thought to apply not only to all organisms, including human beings, but also to society, science, and the earth as a whole. It is a developmental necessarianism in Spencer's sense, which is to say that it is neither an accident nor a thing within human control but rather a beneficent necessity. This idea of a general recapitulation in the form of a law of development seems to be accepted by Piaget and is the fundamental assumption of his theory. His empirical studies of children are offered more to illustrate this than to test it. His theory seems to rest on questionable metaphysical assumptions grounded in or inspired by pre-Darwinian biology, and also on questionable views of both individual cognitive and scientific development, views that see these following a single, necessary path, which also eliminates meaning or intentionality from psychology. His theory is therefore not a theory of cognition or the mind.

The two processes of assimilation and accommodation explain change, but not directed change, and concepts like reflective abstraction are equivalent to rationality, thereby assuming what is to be

[9] This problem is further discussed in the next chapter.

explained. Piaget's account of development is a description of the child's changing behaviour in terms of the different sub-parts which, in the aggregate, allow rationality to be described. He has committed the error that William Wundt long ago warned against (see Danziger, 1985) – the tendency of psychologists to use logic and the accepted concepts of science or rationality to characterise behaviour, and then to transfer this same logical language to the level of psychological mechanisms as well.

Piaget, in insisting that development occurs necessarily along a single path, also has to claim that the entire process of development from infancy to scientific reasoning is fixed in a way that is prior to any experience or constructive mental or other activity. It is not, however, fixed in the individual's genetic endowment, but rather due to some universal biological laws governing all life, and largely independent of social, cultural, or historical facts. Create a natural learning situation and the rest will take care of itself. 'The fundamental hypothesis of genetic epistemology is that there is a parallelism between the progress made in the logical and rational organisation of knowledge and the corresponding formative psychological processes' (Piaget, 1970, p. 3).

Although Piaget claims we cannot predict scientific change, he thinks it is always possible to account for it as a necessary aspect of development after the fact. Again, this supports the claim that all he is doing is re-describing rationality, not explaining its development.

Individual development and the way children learn have adult thinking as their goal, but is this a process similar to the infinite and unpredictable growth of scientific knowledge? Are there really both an indisputable connection and a parallelism between individual development towards adult norms and the growth of science?

To conclude, clearly Piaget thinks that the productivity of cognitive change can be explained in terms of the productivity and normativity of evolutionary laws, in the form of functional invariants of development. This is unsatisfactory because he 'solves' the problem of productivity by creating an analogous one – the productivity and normativity of biological laws of evolution. Clearly this begs the question, because it assumes that reason evolves progressively. But this is the very point that needs to be addressed, rather than assumed. The laws of development would seem to be Piaget's basic assumption, one which he does not argue for and which he characterises as a process of equilibrium, functional invariants, reflective abstraction, and homeostasis. As noted, this adds nothing to our knowledge, but is just re-description of this very assumption. Therefore I would argue that Piaget is committing an error, which is based on the tendency of psychologists to use logic to characterise behaviour, and so transfer this same logical language to the level of psychological mechanisms.

Metaphysical history

Piaget fails to account for productivity, that is, the normativity of cognitive development, the steady progress in the individual as well as in science towards objectivity and certainty, because he presupposes what he sets out to explain, namely rationality. His answer, or rather his failure to give an account for progressive cognitive change, only makes sense if we put it in the context of a set of ideas which were widespread among intellectuals in the nineteenth and early twentieth centuries, and which were alluded to above. The idea of a necessary progression as an assumption of any theory of development cannot be presupposed because it is itself in need of explanation. Piaget's theory thus fits with his acceptance of recapitulation, his claim of the necessity of cognitive development, and his belief that developmental higher-level or transcending laws of evolution direct this progressive development (see for example Messerly, 1996; Morss, 1990; Rotman, 1977; and Russell, 1978). It is in this sense that Piaget is more of a nineteenth-century than a contemporary thinker. He, like Spencer, Bergson, Hegel, Marx, Comte, and Freud, adopts an evolutionary perspective. Although they were interested in different aspects of the individual or society, they all shared the belief that life in all its manifestations – from the amoeba to human cognition to society and cultures – evolves according to laws and that evolution moves in a necessary and progressive direction. This assumption or presupposition is sometimes referred to as either metaphysical history (Scott Gordon, 1991) or historicism (Mandelbaum, 1971; Popper, 1957). The term 'metaphysical history' captures the idea best, I think, because it makes clear that the supposition referred to is a metaphysical one: it understands development in terms of an 'essential nature' rather than 'appearance', that is, necessary rather than contingent. Piaget's basic orientation was clearly evolutionary in this sense. For him, reality in all its forms – the physical, biological, psychological, social, and intellectual – is evolving progressively. Piaget takes external behaviour and different organic and societal manifestations to be contingent, while the functional invariants or evolutionary laws are part of an 'essential nature', rather than an 'appearance'.

CONCLUSION: NATURAL LEARNING AND PRODUCTIVITY

As we have seen above, Piaget's theory is used to support computer use in schools by claiming that children have a natural, inborn motivation and ability to learn. As long as this inborn motivation and these inborn capacities to develop operate freely, children will learn. Just claiming that learning something is natural according to biological laws, as Piaget does, does not help us. To claim that the process is in accordance with natural evolutionary laws is problematic, as I have argued. It says nothing about what this process is like and what influences it. These accounts of learning and cognitive development seem to be traceable to untenable, arguable, metaphysical assumptions which go back to the beginning of psychology, and include assumptions about evolution rejected by neo-Darwinians.

In the end Piaget and the natural learning theorists who rely on him seem to accept the very thing he criticises traditional epistemological theories for. Objectivity, truth, and necessity are the starting points rather than the end point of development. This is so because Piaget finds necessity in developmental biological laws which are 'guiding' all change. Although he is correct to criticise empiricism and rationalism for their static view of knowledge, in the end he is unable to provide an acceptable alternative because he also seems to accept static foundations as a basis of knowledge. To a certain extent, he accepts as well their view that knowledge is generated or has its basis in the individual's internal, private mental and biological abilities. I think that this idea of internalism and individualism is at the root of another of Piaget's failures. Standards and norms are not private, individual entities, but social and cultural ones, thus external to and ordering, rather than being ordered by, the individual's biological and mental endowments. Thus Piaget's failure to address the social and cultural origin of reason itself is problematic. This becomes even clearer in his account of the framework, the topic to which we turn in the next chapter.

4 Piaget's conception of the framework: from instincts to intentionality

Natural learning theories approach the second problem of learning, that is, the problem of the framework, in fundamentally the same way as they approach that of productivity: by focusing on individual, biologically grounded mental states and processes. In order to learn something and to go beyond experience and the information given, the child has to be able to make sense of what he or she encounters, sort out the irrelevant from the relevant, and make it fit with what is already known. What is to be learned has to be meaningful to the learner. This is the case whether productivity is defined as a product of induction, deduction, or what Piaget calls assimilation and accommodation. In order to learn something, the learner has to have a meaningful framework into which new experiences are fitted. How is this basic framework, which enables all subsequent learning, acquired? How do natural learning theories account for this? Again, my discussion focuses on Piaget, but before turning to a discussion of his ideas, some general points about mental activity and meaning need to be made. I shall also briefly mention Chomsky's solution to the problem of the framework. Since the same criticisms that I use to evaluate Piaget's views can be used to assess Chomsky's basic assumption, I shall not repeat them again here.[1]

The intentionality of mental frameworks
Mental operations or mental states like thinking and believing are different from physical states and events. The most important

---

[1] For a discussion of Chomsky's and Fodor's account of the framework, see Erneling (1993). Piaget is, though, correct in his criticism of Chomsky for having a too static view of knowledge and its growth.

difference in this context is that mental states or processes are intentional and have meaning for the person who has them. They are states that are experienced as being directed at something other than themselves. When we think about a unicorn or see a horse or believe it is going to rain tomorrow, the content of our thoughts is about something other than themselves, namely the unicorn, the horse, and the rain. Our thoughts point beyond themselves by providing representations and having meaning. Beliefs and other mental states or propositional attitudes are directed at real or imagined events or objects, that is, something other than the individual's mental content; they are about the world, imagined or real. Any theory of the mental has to say something about the relationship between thought and the world, and how the contents of thoughts refer to and represent something outside themselves. How is it that the contents of mental attitudes have meaning, that is, refer to and represent something outside themselves? This is one of the central and most difficult problems in accounting for thinking and cognition (see Erneling and Erneling, 2005) and has to be addressed in any account of the framework of learning (see Erneling, 1993), since a meaningful framework is the precondition for all learning. Natural learning theories, like Piaget's, approach this in the same way as does the mainstream 'ideal of psychological order', focusing on the child's individual innate or constructed framework. The child is seen as a Robinson Crusoe figure constructing his or her own meaning, who then moves outwards from private thoughts and connects them with what other people in the surrounding cognitive and linguistic community are saying and doing.

The initial natural framework

As we have seen above, the natural learning position stresses the biological nature and often even the innateness of cognitive abilities. One very important reason for assuming that mental capabilities and learning have an innate base comes not only from empirical studies or general biological claims, but also from philosophical arguments claiming that the innateness position is the only tenable one. This argument goes back to Plato and has been called Meno's paradox. This paradox, as I explained in Chapter 1, refers to the idea that in order to learn something one already has to know it, and in this sense all learning is re-collection or re-presentation, thus not really learning. Accepting this, both the linguist Chomsky and the philosopher Fodor (see for example Piattelli-Palmarini, 1980, p. 260) claim that it is a logical truth or tautology that children are innately equipped with symbols and mental representations. In Chomsky's case, the initial framework consists of an innate universal grammar, and in Fodor's case, of an innate language of thought that contains all concepts necessary to form hypotheses in order to learn all other concepts.

Piaget challenges this for the same reason that he challenges traditional accounts of productivity, namely because they fail to account for the basic active constructive processes of cognition. He claims that children, through increased use of reflexes and sensorimotor activity (that is, purely physical interaction with the environment like grasping, banging, pulling), and through the imitation of their own behaviour as well as that of others, gain the ability to engage in symbolic or representational activity. Learning concepts like causality, movement, mind, etc., as well as a natural language, are based on this mimetic-representational activity, which first is executed physically and later internalised as mental representational or symbolic activity or thought. This initial mental framework is then the basis for all later cognitive development.

Piaget firmly defends the view that children are born as natural beings exhibiting specific reflexes but lacking mind and cognition. Children are not born believing or thinking, but become believers and thinkers in their second year when they have acquired the ability to re-present the world around them mentally, that is, when they have the basic framework of meaning upon which all subsequent cognitive development rests. This, he claims, is the basis of the acquisition of language and other cognitive abilities. Thus, both thought and language are the outcome of biological processes which do not involve thought. By employing this approach, Piaget attempts to avoid a

serious problem, namely that in order to explain thinking and cognitive activity one has to assume cognition, and in this way he hopes to
overcome Meno's paradox. But as we shall see, he fails because his
account of the intentionality or meaningfulness of the initial mental
framework fails. It fails because, in common with his account of the
productivity of cognitive development, he seems to presuppose what
he intends to explain.

THE EMERGENCE OF INTENTIONALITY FROM PURELY REFLECTIVE BEHAVIOUR

As we have seen, for Piaget all cognition and learning are instances of
biological adaptations. At birth, the child is a purely biological being
whose behaviour and adaptation to the environment is dependent upon
its instincts. These instincts are the initial framework that makes all
later cognition and learning possible. That is, intentional, productive,
and normative mental states and processes develop out of these non-
mental ways of interacting with the environment. Purely sensori-
motor action is the basis for the development around the child's second
year of operational or representative and meaningful thinking. Even if
interaction with the environment changes with representational
thinking and something new is achieved by the developing individual,
there is a functional continuity between early, non-mental adaptations
and later mental ones, because the same process of equilibration
applies to both. As I discussed in Chapter 3, successive stages of
equilibration lead to increasingly stable mental schemas and are the
result of assimilation and accommodation of earlier schemas.

   In spite of a functional continuity, the transition taking place at
the end of the sensori-motor period around two years of age is a crucial
one. It is the introduction of the mental or the mind into the natural
world. It begins when the child has acquired symbolic mental representations of the world, that is, when the child has meaningful mental
states directed at or representing something other than himself or
herself. In Piaget's terminology, the child has now acquired mental
operations.

So what is involved in the child's acquisition of the ability to re-present, according to Piaget? It involves two different aspects. First, the child has to master the ability to use one thing – an object, sign, or symbol (linguistic or other) – to stand for or re-present something other than itself. Second, the child, if he or she wants to use his or her re-presentational ability to communicate with others, has to acquire the conventional meanings of words or symbols used in the cognitive and linguistic community the child is surrounded by. Piaget seems to think that the first ability, to represent – or rather re-present – something, is fundamental to thought such that when the child has internalised representational activity the child is a thinking being, a being with mental states. With this initial mental framework in place, the child can go on to develop more and more advanced cognitive activities and schemas. The learning of conventional meaning is then just a match-ing of internal private symbols with public, conventional, and social signs.

The ability to represent is based on two skills, imitation and play, which develop during the child's first year. These skills, however, are meta-skills since they employ most of the child's sensori-motor skills in a special way. They constitute a skilful way of using skills or a set of skills which are then applied to another set of skills. In imitation, the child matches his or her sensori-motor skills to external examples of the same behaviour; in the beginning, the child's own behaviour, but later that of other people or objects. The child begins to imitate other persons' behaviour quite early, and later, around the end of the sensori-motor period, imitation moves from behaviour and becomes internal-ised. One quite well-known illustration of what happens when the child is in the process of internalising imitations as re-presentations is the case of one of Piaget's own children, who was engaged in trying to get a bracelet out of a partly closed match box (see for example Piaget, 1936/1963). Trying different physical manipulations like shaking etc., she suddenly stopped and opened and closed her mouth, and then she opened the box. Here Piaget sees in the opening and closing of her mouth the physical imitation of a physical action executed earlier which is then carried out. The child is able to represent physically to herself an action that she has already performed in other contexts and to use it as a representation to guide her behaviour, which is then executed. When such actions are internalised, the child has mental representations and is a thinking being. Representing is literally re-presenting, that is, the presentation of a copy of something else, which will be associated later with a public sign, in this case 'open'.[2]

Furthermore, imitation is a prerequisite for play, especially for pretend or symbolic play, which has a crucial role in developing intentionality or semantic skills, skills by which one makes sense of experiences. Play, like imitation, is the use of already mastered skills in a different context. Beginning as pure practice play or the repetition of sensori-motor activities, it becomes symbolic or pretend play in the year-old infant. The child masters pretend play, and then he or she is capable of deferred imitation, that is, the imitation of earlier actions, events, or observed objects at a later time. For example, one of Piaget's own children coming home from her daycare centre one day started to scream and kick without any apparent reason or without being angry or upset. She was not expressing her own emotions but rather imitating the behaviour of a boy at the daycare centre. Pretending that a stick is a horse or a piece of cloth a pillow are other examples of play, in which an object is used to re-present something other than itself. In many cases, both imitation and play modify the 'original' behaviour, as for example when a behaviour sequence is not performed in full or is simplified.

Imitation and play both require skills over and above purely sensori-motor ones. This is so because both imitation and play are skilful activities involving displacement or re-presentation, that is, the use of activities, events, objects, etc. not present. In this respect, they present the germ of the 'idea' that actions, objects, and eventually words can represent, signify, or symbolise something other than themselves. The internalisation of these acts of play and imitation is the

---

[2] See Donald (1991) for a more contemporary example of a mimesis theory of thought and language.

beginning of mental activity and intentionality. Imitation and play are intrinsically motivating for infants, and infants engage in them without the encouragement of adults, according to Piaget. Furthermore, children develop these meta-skills by actively interacting with the environment on their own. Here we see the typical characteristics of all learning, according to natural learning theories. It is active, individual, and inherently motivating, and the role of other human beings like parents or teachers is minimal.

The meaningfulness of early pre-linguistic mental re-presentations

Piaget claims that what the child internalises in mental imitation are images of his or her own activity, of objects, or a combination of both. These images are idiosyncratic and have no conventional or public meaning, yet they are assumed to be meaningful and representational. They are intentional and hence provide the child with his or her initial framework on which all subsequent cognitive and linguistic development rests.

What makes such an internalised image a representation of something? What confers meaning on it? Is it the child who by means of a mental act gives it meaning, or is it something in the image itself which carries its own meaning, as it were? It is clear that Piaget favours the second alternative. In one of his early books, *The Origins of Intelligence* (1936/1963), he describes the emergence of representation and thinking in the sixth and last of the sensori-motor stages during the child's second year. He describes what happens with the invention of new means (for action) through mental combinations of images which are representations of actions, objects, or both in combination. 'Images are … simply the tools of nascent thought' and 'The image so constituted therefore becomes the signifier' (1936/1963, p. 353). These images are never exact copies of actions or of objects because the child assimilates incoming stimuli to already established action schemes, which in their turn are changed or accommodated to the new information. Nevertheless, they are representations by virtue of their resemblance to what they represent. They are 'modelled increasingly on the characteristics of things and so tend to form images' (1936/1963, p. 355). Piaget's example of the opening and closing of the mouth as a representation of the action to open the box also illustrates this.

The idea that images represent by virtue of their resemblance becomes even more pronounced in later works like *Play, Dreams, and Imagination in Childhood* (1945/1962). Here he deals with the issue of the emergence of representation more explicitly. For example, he claims that there is representation when an absent model is imitated: 'the child becomes capable of imitating internally a series of models in the form of images or suggestions of actions' (Piaget, 1945/1962, p. 62).

Piaget describes these representational internal images as symbols which are related to the signified by some resemblance, as opposed to conventional or arbitrary signs. Thus 'the symbol is "motivated", *i.e.*, there is resemblance between "signifier" and signified' (Piaget, 1945/1962, p. 98; see also pp. 68 and 99–100).

In discussing the emergence of symbolic or pretend play, the idea of representation as resemblance re-emerges in Piaget's discussion when he makes a distinction between symbol and sign. The symbol, on the other hand, depends on resemblance between the present object, which Piaget calls the 'signifier', and the 'signified': 'But, as we know, the "sign" is "arbitrary" or conventional, while the symbol is motivated, *i.e.*, there is resemblance between "signifier" and "signified"' (Piaget, 1945/1962, p. 98).

In *Play, Dreams, and Imagination in Childhood*, the pre-linguistic and non-social nature of representation and thinking is clearly stated, as well as the idea that private symbols are the basis of language acquisition. For example, 'the acquisition of language is itself subordinated to the working of the symbolic function' (Piaget, 1945/1962, p. 1). And furthermore 'Though obviously social life plays an essential role in the elaboration of concepts and of the representational schemes ... it does not in itself explain the beginnings of the image or the symbol' (Piaget, 1945/1962, p. 4). The symbolic function is considered 'as an individual mechanism whose existence is a pre-requisite for interaction of thought between individuals and conse-quently for the constitution or acquisition of collective meanings' (1945/1962, p. 4). And 'We must, however, point to an essential differ-ence between the symbol as represented by the image and the social signs of language. The mental image remains individual, ... [it] is only a translation of personal experiences' (1945/1962, p. 71).

Although Piaget modifies his theories of cognitive development in various respects, his ideas on representation and intentionality remain the same. In the collections of essays incorporated in the volume *Sociological Studies* (1950/1965/1995), he expresses the same view in those essays which cover the period 1928–51. In 1933 he claims that the symbol will be created by the individual's assimilating an absent object to present experience, by endowing the object with some link of resemblance to the experience. Furthermore, 'The symbol is thus the instrument of individual thought *par excellence*' (Piaget, 1950/1965/1995, p. 224). In 1950 he writes: 'The individual *qua* indi-vidual, i.e. independently of all interaction with others, is able to create "symbols" by means of resemblance between the signified and the signifier ... The sign, in contrast, is arbitrary and therefore presupposes a convention' (1950/1965/1995, pp. 44–5).

Let me now summarise Piaget's views. He clearly states that the child first, in advance of and as a condition for the acquisition of language, acquires an internal, private representational framework, which literally mentally re-presents an external object, action, or event, or aspects of them.

Here his views are very much in line with both traditional philosophy and psychology.[3] In fundamental respects Piaget's views are not very different from the idea of a language of thought presented by Jerry Fodor (1975/1979). They also resemble those of the early Wittgenstein and are therefore firmly entrenched in philosophy as well. In the *Tractatus Logico-Philosophicus* (1961), Wittgenstein was

---

[3] See for example Erneling (1993).

trying to solve the problem of what relationship one fact – a representation – has to have to another fact – the thing, event, or aspect it represents – in order to be a symbol of the latter. His answer is that thought itself is intrinsically meaningful due to the fact that it is isomorphic with (1961 , 2.2., 2.16), or shares logical form with, what it depicts or refers to. It is self-illuminating by containing its own method of representation, or, put another way, it is meaningful by virtue of its internal structure. Among other things, this appears to lead to (methodological) solipsism and the idea that the person is a prisoner of his or her own language of thought. This is also exactly how Piaget describes both the 'autistic' infant and 'the egocentric child': the child lacks objectivity and is a prisoner of his or her own point of view. Piaget's initial mental framework is in line with the traditional Cartesian–Kantian view of mind and meaning. Instead of escaping or transcending – to borrow a term from Thomas Nagel (1995) – the egocentric predicament of Western philosophy, Piaget is a prisoner of it. By 'the egocentric predicament' Nagel is referring to one of the central themes of Western philosophy: the suspicion that we are trapped inside our mind and neither language, thought, imagination, nor perception will allow us to go beyond it. Intentionality and representational thinking – a meaningful framework – are something the individual develops on his or her own, from his or her own individual constructive activity, according to Piaget.

This similarity to Wittgenstein's early theories also extends to Piaget's account of the acquisition of a public language. On the basis of the private symbolic representation, the child learns the public language. Piaget's account is fundamentally the same as the one Wittgenstein quotes from St Augustine in section 1 of the *Philosophical Investigations*; it is 'as if the child came into a strange country and did not understand the language of the country; that is, as if it already had a language, but not this one. Or again: as if the child could already *think*, only not yet speak' (Wittgenstein, 1953, sec. 32).

The later Wittgenstein rejected his own earlier account of meaning, so I shall proceed to use his arguments along with others to expose problems in Piaget's account.[4]

Problems with Piaget's account of intentionality

Resemblance

Piaget claims that a mental symbol 'represents' by virtue of being similar to what it represents. But similarity or resemblance is neither necessary nor sufficient for representation. It is not necessary because gestures and signs not resembling something are representational; e.g., most symbols, like words, do not resemble what they refer to. But neither is it sufficient, because as Putnam (1981) points out, a trace made by some ants in the sand resembling Churchill is not a representation of Churchill. For something to be a symbol or representation of something it has to be taken as such, that is, it has to be intended as a symbol or meant to be a symbolic representation. An example is the case of Wittgenstein's stick figure, which could be interpreted as going up or down a hill, or going sideways, or being immobile. The image has to be interpreted, intended, or meant (Wittgenstein, 1953, p. 54). But intention or meaning are the very notions we want to explain, hence referring to them is like going in a circle, that is, we have explained nothing.

Yet another problem is that anything can be taken to resemble anything else depending on how we interpret or use it. A hammer can be used to symbolise a chair, or a table to symbolise the ocean. There is no natural way to determine resemblance. One has to ask in what respect something resembles something else, and this depends on the context or use of the symbol (see for example Wittgenstein, 1953, sec. 48). But might not Piaget reply that the child's mental images are indeed understood in a context, namely the child's own private sensori-motor schema? They thus have a resemblance for the child but not for anybody else. But as we have seen, the similarity cited

---

[4] See Erneling (1993).

above is neither sufficient nor necessary for making something a symbol or representation of something else, so this response has not helped Piaget at all.

We seem to be left with the claim that for something to represent something it has to be intended as a representation, and Piaget sometimes writes as if this were the case. When Piaget speaks about representation, he also speaks about the act of physical or mental imitation being involved. Is this a hint that meaning is conferred by a mental act, namely that it is interpreted or intended to be the same? The child creates a symbol by endowing it with the assumption of resemblance.

Here as well Wittgenstein can be used to expose the difficulty. Arguing against the school of act psychology (see Bloor, 1983; Erneling, 1993), Wittgenstein claimed that the mental act of intention was as mysterious as that which it is supposed to explain: 'For neither the expression "to intend a definition in such-and-such a way" nor the expression "to interpret the definition in such-and-such a way" stands for a process which accompanies the giving and hearing of a definition' (Wittgenstein, 1953, sec. 34). The same point comes up in Wittgenstein's discussion of understanding (1953, secs. 138, 140, 151–5, 186–8). To understand something meaningfully is not to be guided by some strange process or mental act. No new act of meaning is required in every use of a symbol.

To conclude: to account for meaning and intentionality either in terms of resemblance between a mental image or representation and what it refers to, or in terms of intending to re-present, is problematic. It seems to lack explanatory value and, just as in the case of productivity, moves the problem to another level. This mental level is, then, in as much need of explanation as the level of behaviour at which Piaget began.

Non-social origin of intentionality

As we have already seen, Piaget stresses that one of the crucial differences between a symbol and a sign is that the first is individual and private, without connection to a public language or any shared activity, while the second – the sign – is not. 'The individual *qua* individual, i.e. independently of all interaction with others, is able to create "symbols" by means of resemblance between the signified and the signifier' (Piaget, 1950/1965/1995, pp. 44–5).

Symbolisation appears here as some kind of private naming. The view expressed by Piaget closely resembles Augustine's view quoted at the beginning of Wittgenstein's *Philosophical Investigations*, and the same objections presented against it apply to Piaget's account. Wittgenstein speaks about sensations, but the same criticism applies to mental images. Wittgenstein thinks that the account of the child in naming his or her own mental sensations or images is not intelligible by presupposing an inner process of private ostension, that is, naming something by 'pointing' to it (1953 secs. 243, 257).

The first problem with private ostension is the difficulty in the child's knowing what to look for in his or her inner stream of consciousness: how does the child know that this sensation is 'pain' or that image, using an invented word, is 'tove'? Furthermore, even if the child could somehow identify the referent of what he or she him- or herself has named 'pain' or 'tove', he or she does not know whether 'pain' refers to the unpleasantness, the sharpness of the sensation, or if 'tove' refers to the colour, shape or texture of the image of the tove. Wittgenstein writes 'a great deal of stage setting in the language is presupposed if the mere act of naming is to make sense. And when we speak of someone's having given a name to pain, what is presupposed is the existence of a grammar of the word "pain"; it shews the post where the new word is stationed' (1953, sec. 257).

But let us grant Piaget the claim that the child somehow has managed this seemingly impossible task. Perhaps his or her sensori-motor schemes provide the required signposts. But even if he or she succeeds in this naming of a sensation or an image, one can still ask 'Does this mean that the child understands the symbol when the child has impressed on itself the connection between the private name of the symbol and the image or sensation?' (1953, sec. 258). Wittgenstein's point is that even if one has named a sensation or image at one time, at a later date when one wants to identify it as the same sensation or image, the previous sensation or image is not before one's mind. In addition, the memory image of it could be mistaken, since one has no way of telling the difference between two or more sensations or images appearing and actually being the same. Thus there is no difference between applying the symbol rightly or wrongly, which is the same as saying there is no naming.

Even if all these objections could be overcome and the child could know in his or her own case what 'pain' or 'tove' means, he or she still could not know what someone else means by them. This means that communication about pain is an illusion, since the referent is private for each person. Even worse, the referent to the word 'pain' becomes irrelevant in speaking about pains, because it could refer to different things or nothing at all for different people. The same is true in the case of 'tove'. Thus, the private sensation or image is an idle postulation or reification; the machinery could not be run with it and clearly runs without it. The step of postulating a mental image or symbol, as Piaget does, only creates confusion. Mental images exist, but they do not have the explanatory power Piaget gives them, so they cannot function as symbols.

This brings me to the next objection: mental images do not enable the child to communicate with others and break out of its egocentric predicament. Although Piaget denies social interaction a role in acquiring intentionality, he has to leave room for later social influences. Learning natural language benefits from others' experience, and all later learning in school and other contexts require the ability to communicate.

According to Piaget's view, which accords with the traditional view in philosophy, words are meaningful because of their relationship to mental images or acts, which are prior to language. The word 'brick' refers to the material object via an image or symbol for which 'brick' stands. But how is this new connection between public words and the private images or symbols established? Piaget says hardly anything about it, but he seems to imply that it is a process of translation, as in the case of learning a foreign language when one already has a language.

There are at least two ways of understanding this process of translation: either as a process of understanding or grasping, or as a 'mechanical translation', as it were. Wittgenstein has pointed out problems with both these interpretations. Understanding is not a state or process (Wittgenstein, 1953, sec. 149; see also secs. 152, 154, or 153), but a public activity that varies with context.

The mechanical process of translation, which entails connecting the private symbol with the public sign, is not a mental process either. Wittgenstein uses the same method mentioned above to expose problems here. He replaces the mysterious process of mental translation with 'mechanical reading'. He then argues that just as reading is not sensation because there is no characteristic sensation of reading (1953, secs. 159, 165, 168), although it involves the brain it is not a brain process, because we do not need to know the brain process in making justifiable claims that someone is reading; nor is it a process of being guided by derivation from the private symbol, because then the sign would have to contain its own rule of application or translation. This leads to an infinite regress of rules interpreting rules (1953, p. 54 and sec. 19). Thus it seems that the postulation of private mental symbols fails and does not help us to understand how public language is acquired.

In conclusion: in the last section of part 1 of *Philosophical Investigations* Wittgenstein says 'And nothing is more wrong-headed than calling meaning a mental activity! Unless, that is, one is setting out to produce confusion' (1953, sec. 693). And confusion is just what Piaget creates in his discussion of the acquisition of the initial mental framework. As characterised by Piaget, it does not make sense and cannot function as the building block for later cognitive development. This is so because he assumes, along with traditional views in philosophy and psychology, that intentionality and representation can be accounted for in terms of individual behaviours and the internalisation of these in the form of mental images. Instead, the capacity to think meaningfully requires something outside the individual child. The mental framework is divided into individual skills – the first being to use something to re-present something, and the second being to do this in accordance with public rules – and here Piaget is correct. Where he is mistaken is in not seeing that the first of these skills – representation or meaning and intentionality – requires a framework that is external to the individual.

CONCLUSION: PIAGET'S FAILURE TO ACCOUNT FOR BOTH PRODUCTIVITY AND THE FRAMEWORK

Piaget's starting point for his theory of cognitive development – and his proposed solution to the problems posed by the issues of productivity and the framework of learning – is his endeavour to replace traditional rationalist and empiricist assumptions. He replaces them with an account of cognitive and scientific development which assumes that objectivity, conceptual compulsion, truth, and certainty are the end products of a process that in a fundamental sense rests on biological invariants or laws of development. This attempt, as we have seen above, is problematic. He ends up with a position that is very similar to the traditions he set out to replace. He attempts to solve the problem of both meaningfulness and productivity of the framework by reference to individual private processes of biological origin, which already contain what he wants to explain – namely productivity and meaning. Thus, his views are similar to both empiricism and rationalism, in the sense that certainty or meaning are both given, rather than the result of construction. In rationalism and empiricism, necessity and certainty are the characteristics of innate ideas or sense impressions; for Piaget, they are the characteristics of evolutionary or developmental laws.

As has been indicated above, I think this failure is mainly the result of Piaget's attempt to trace the basis of cognition to the biology of individual mental processes. By disregarding the argument that thinking and its development in the individual and in science are a result of both biologically based individual skills *and* social and cultural practices, he fails. Piaget shares his failure with the mainstream 'ideal of psychological order'. In Chapter 6 I present an alternative to these approaches. As indicated in Chapter 1, there are two main approaches to cognition and learning in psychology: the mainstream and the social discourse approach. My focus in presenting and discussing the social discourse alternative will take as its basis a discussion of language acquisition, because most natural learning theories take this as the paradigm case of natural learning. As we have seen in Chapter 2, this is clearly the case with natural learning theories concerned with the educational use of computers. With this as a basis, I argue that Piaget, natural learning theories, and the mainstream 'ideal of psychological order' share a mistaken and excessively narrow conception of the mental, because they restrict it to individual and inner mental processes.

Before doing this, I want to discuss an instance of the claim that infant learning is the paradigm case of learning, namely Gopnik and Meltzoff's (1997) assertion, developing and partly going beyond Piaget's views, that infants think, act, and learn in the same way as scientists. Papert also makes such a claim (see Chapter 2) in his promotion of the educational value of computer technology. These claims rest upon a mistaken conception of mind and mental activity as well as a mistaken conception of knowledge. This is a conception of knowledge and mind which is also shared by Piaget.

5 The infant as scientist

INTRODUCTION

In Chapter 2 we saw how Seymour Papert in particular compared infant learning to learning in school and to scientific activity. The idea of comparing children with scientists goes back to Piaget, but has moved beyond his initial interest in the matter. One of Piaget's strongest motivations, if not the strongest, for studying intellectual development in children was to get a better grasp of scientific reasoning (see for example Piaget, 1970, p. 1). Even more important was the fact that in his genetic epistemology, he took science as the paradigm form of knowledge. Furthermore, his view that all knowledge acquisition is determined by the same biological laws, and his belief in the process of equilibration through assimilation and accommodation, set the foundations for a continuity between cognitive development and science. In addition, Chomsky's view of language acquisition as hypothesis testing gave further credence to the idea of children as small scientists (Leudar and Costall, 2004; Leudar, Costall, and Francis, 2004). This conception of cognition has had a profound influence on contemporary psychology, resulting in what is known as the 'theory theory' and the 'theory of mind' approaches, and is also found in some versions of evolutionary psychology. These have become some of the central and fastest-growing areas in psychology, and would deserve a book (or several) of their own. Let me, however, focus on some problems which are more immediately relevant to my overall argument. Mainstream psychology overlooks the fundamental socio-cultural aspect of mental activity, namely the fact that the framework for learning is both public and collective in its ordering of individual mental activity. 'Theory of theory' as well as 'theory of mind' approaches do not deny that humans

Part of this chapter is an adaptation of a paper in Emeling and Johnson, 2005.

are in important aspects social beings and provide social linguistic explanations, yet these theories' conception of 'social' is explicated in terms of individual beliefs and mental mechanisms, thus making them part of what I call the mainstream 'ideal of psychological order' (see for example Astington and Baird, 2005; Gopnik, 2009).

I start my discussion of the fundamental assumptions of these approaches by discussing one of the first systematic and comprehensive accounts, namely *Words, Thoughts, and Theories* (1997) by Alison Gopnik and Andrew N. Meltzoff. The authors have since modified their views (Gopnik, 2004, 2009; Meltzoff and Prinz, 2002), but the basic assumptions about knowledge and science and the accompanying Cartesian assumptions remain (see Gopnik, 2004; see also Gopnik, Meltzoff and Kuhl, 1999). After discussing their views, I will briefly address some assumptions of the so-called 'theory of mind' approach to children's social cognition, in particular the idea that children are small social scientists or psychologists. My aim is not to give a comprehensive discussion of this body of research, but rather to show how it is related to assumptions made by natural learning theories and to discuss some of their problematic aspects. The discussion also prepares the way for my argument in the next chapter.

In *Words, Thoughts, and Theories* (1997), Gopnik and Meltzoff go beyond Piaget's claim that the child is actively and intelligently exploring its world, and claim that the child is thinking and acting just like a scientist. Like the scientist the child creates, tests, and revises theories. In fact, the child in this respect surpasses the normal adult, who is portrayed as a much duller creature. In spite of this difference, Piaget and these authors share the same mistaken view of knowledge and of cognition.

Simply stated, Gopnik and Meltzoff's comparison between scientific activity and cognitive activity in children is based on a misleading conception of knowledge. As a result, the authors fail to provide a satisfactory account of the growth of knowledge both in science and in the child. Their failure is not primarily a result of inadequate empirical studies or a lack of them, but rather of conceptual confusion about what science, knowledge, and cognition involve. This difficulty is endemic to mainstream psychology, and to Piaget and other natural learning theorists, as well as to the so-called 'theory of mind' paradigm and evolutionary psychology.

This conceptual confusion is related to the more fundamental issue of the ontological commitment or 'ideal of psychological order' of the authors and developmental psychologists, which in fundamental respects is Cartesian. The Cartesian ontology of the mental rests on two main assumptions. The first is that the body and mind are different substances, and the second is the 'atomistic assumption' that the basic entities or units of cognition are individualised states of 'mind-stuff', and as such are properties of particular persons. They assume that cognitive representations and norms, both in science and in children, are private mental states of individual brains. I think this last assumption is the most problematic. The trouble is that, as van Gelder (2005) argues, there is a large class of mental states, e.g., beliefs, which cannot be individuated, in the sense of being understood to be occurring in the brains of individual human beings, but can only be understood as 'immanent', that is, in normatively ordered and dynamic public contexts.

CHILDREN AND SCIENCE: THE GROWTH OF KNOWLEDGE

The authors' fundamental claim is that infants as young as nine months are miniature theoreticians and scientists, creating, testing, and sometimes changing theories about the world and about other people. Children have and use theories of objects, of actions, and of how other people think and feel. The authors call theirs the 'theory theory', because it is a theory about children's theories. Infants and young children do not start with the knowledge or theories that adults or scientists have, but neither do they start with reflexes as Piaget claimed. Instead they are born equipped with some innate responses and a propensity to make false recognitions. As the authors put it, children have theories which are both specific and false, as well as an ability to test, reject, and form new theories. In this fundamental way, children are not only as rational as scientists, but even outstrip the everyday activities of normal adults.[1]

Obviously, scientific knowledge cannot grow unless there are individual scientists using their cognitive abilities. And equally unquestionably, the acquisition of knowledge in children involves the use of individual cognitive abilities. But the authors are more specific than this and argue that the processes that lead to the growth of scientific knowledge are the very same ones found in infants. Thus their arguments are a more developed version of the claims made by Seymour Papert in conjunction with his argument for the use of computers in schools (see Chapter 2).

In asserting a fundamental similarity between scientific activity and the way children reason, Gopnik and Meltzoff opt for what they call the cognitive view of science, namely that cognitive changes in the minds of individual scientists provide at least a partial explanation of scientific growth (Gopnik and Meltzoff, 1997, p. 14). Scientists and their cognitive activity are a necessary though not a sufficient condition for producing scientific knowledge, to be sure, but the authors seem to assume that the cognitive activity of scientists alone is both necessary and sufficient. While individual cognitive processes are involved in scientific activity, these same processes or abilities also establish limits to such activity. Thus to propose rules and methodologies for science which are not compatible with human cognitive functioning is bound to fail. But this is a long way from claiming that theoretical change in science is something which is based only on the private, subjective conviction of the individual scientist, and thus found in the cognitive structures of individuals. Yet this is what the

---

[1] Their assertion about a lack of intellectual activity in adults is mysterious, and I can understand it only as a way of claiming that adults are normally less engaged in intellectual activity than children and scientists. Adults are too busy with more mundane things, like caring for their scientist-children, as the authors point out. I do not think they can seriously maintain that there is any qualitative difference between the intellect of adults and that of children and scientists, only that they as a group are less interesting to study, given the authors' problem context. This is evident later on in the book, when they repeatedly compare children's and adults' reasoning processes.

authors do (Gopnik and Meltzoff, 1997, p. 7). They claim that the most important aspect of scientific activity is the psychological activity of individual scientists who create, test, and reject theories. This view falls back on the philosophical tradition represented by philosophers like Francis Bacon and René Descartes. This approach to knowledge and the growth of knowledge assumes scientific growth to be a matter of private experience and certainty. It does not deny social interaction as a part of scientific activity, but it does not take such interaction as a necessary precondition for it.

The authors acknowledge that scientific activity involves specific social settings, which are different from the ones that children find themselves in. But they do not think that such differences are important enough to justify rejecting the comparison they make between children and scientists. On the contrary, they think there is an important social similarity between children and scientists in that both groups have a considerable amount of leisure time (Gopnik and Meltzoff, 1997, p. 25).

The literature in the philosophy and sociology of science over the last century is very diverse, to the point that there seems to be virtually no agreement about what constitutes science. Yet there is general agreement on one thing, namely that the individualistic, 'Robinson Crusoe' view of science from traditional philosophy should be replaced by a social conception of science.[2]

There are two interconnected points to be made here. The first is that contemporary philosophers of science like Karl Popper and Thomas Kuhn agree that the objectivity and creativity of science, which sets it apart from other activities, is based in special social institutions or traditions. For example, Popper (1963) argues that

[2] I focus only on some aspects of these authors' conception of scientific cognition and activity. For example, I assume with them that scientific knowledge is propositional, although this is problematic. It ignores the importance of humans' abilities to construct concrete models in the world and in imagination, which is fundamental to scientific cognition and activity. It also questions Piaget's assumption that scientific thinking, in contrast to children's thinking, is abstract (Harré, personal communication; see also Harré, 2000).

when science first emerged in the Greek pre-Socratic world, dogmatism was replaced by a tradition of critical thinking. This is a new social tradition involving rational interaction, based on free discussion and criticism between pupils and their teachers, and was the engine of the early as well as the contemporary theory of change in science. Of course, critical discussion requires the participation of individual persons, but this critical discussion is made possible by the new attitude and a new cultural setting. Furthermore, it involves public discussion of the content of hypotheses or theories and statements, rather than being a matter of individual cognitive certainty. It is important to note that Popper stresses this public and social critical discussion of hypotheses as scientific. All living organisms in a sense propose hypotheses to the environment, but not all hypotheses are scientific.

Kuhn (1962), although he focuses on more irrational aspects of scientific growth, makes a similar sociological point when he stresses the importance of paradigms, normal science, and scientific revolutions, all of which are social phenomena.

According to both Popper and Kuhn, it is not the specific social arrangements at universities or in laboratories that are important for science, but the general fact that science is a public and social activity of a special kind. In contrast, Gopnik and Meltzoff argue that since Kepler and Newton operated in a very different social setting from that of today's scientists, social arrangements are irrelevant for scientific change and growth, and these authors therefore miss the mark. Contemporary philosophers of science maintain not that it is certain details of the institutional arrangements in themselves that are important, but that the critical tradition (Popper), the presence of paradigms, normal science, and revolutions (Kuhn), all social activities, set science apart. Gopnik and Meltzoff thus misrepresent the view they want to reject. One important reason they do this is based on a confusion of two different meanings of knowledge and knowledge growth. This brings me to my second point.

This point can be stated briefly and simply. Scientific change involves changes in the propositional contents of theories. These contents are not psychological entities but logical-linguistic entities expressed symbolically and publicly in language, in mathematics, and in other ways. Therefore, scientific growth is different from individual cognitive development. By ignoring this difference, Gopnik and Meltzoff fail to appreciate the distinction between two different senses or conceptions of knowledge (see for example Popper, 1972).

Let me explain. The first conception of knowledge addressed by Popper refers to thoughts and theories in the subjective or psychological sense, that is, states of mind or of consciousness, or dispositions to react and behave. The second conception of knowledge refers to knowledge in the objective sense, that is, the propositional content of theories, problems, and arguments. Knowledge in this latter sense is independent of anyone's behaviour or claim to know, although of course human beings do use such knowledge. Popper makes a distinction between the content of a specific proposition and the mental attitude one can have towards this proposition, like believing or accepting it. Another way to state the same distinction is to say that knowledge in the first, subjective sense refers to individual mental processes, while knowledge in the second sense refers to the objective content of these thoughts or mental processes. Popper (1972, p. 109) cites Frege's way of making this distinction as 'I understand by a *thought* not the subjective act of thinking but its *objective content.*'

There is clear evidence in their text that Gopnik and Meltzoff do not make this distinction. In both their descriptions and their explanations of children's behaviour, they move back and forth from one conception of knowledge to the other without appearing to acknowledge the difference. For instance, they discuss (Gopnik and Meltzoff, 1997, p. 3) the process of cognitive development in children and scientists (subjective sense) in one sentence, and in the next they speak about scientific theory change (objective). On page 6 of their work, we find the same pattern: first they refer to cognitive development as knowledge in the subjective sense, and then to theory change, knowledge in the objective sense. On page 19, they discuss scientific representations and rules, and compare them to children's representation and rules. On the previous page (1997, p. 18), they refer to close links between science (objective) and childhood cognition (subjective), and on page 21 to conceptual change in children (subjective) and in science (objective). Furthermore, they describe theory change as cognitive change (1997, p. 39) and even ascribe human-like qualities to theories, as for example when they speak about the advances that a theory makes (1997, p. 100).[3]

Their discussion is confused in much the same way as many contemporary natural learning theories (e.g., Papert's) are. We also find a similar problem in Piaget's writings (see for example Piaget, 1970). This confusion is serious because it obscures the fact that science and scientific change are not an appropriate model for all cognitive development. As already mentioned, science and scientific activity are public activities, which involve changes in the public propositional content of theories, and are not primarily concerned with changing psychological processes, although, of course, changes of this latter sort are involved as well. By using science as their model, the authors are appealing to a non-psychological activity or entity to explain a psychological entity. They are committing what Ryle (1949) called a category mistake. They should have been consistent, comparing the propositional content of the beliefs of scientists and children on the one side, and their respective cognitive capabilities or skills on the other. Occasionally they do this (e.g., Gopnik and Meltzoff, 1997, p. 24), but in every case their comparisons are superficial. For example, children and scientists have the same type of facial expressions when they solve difficult problems; both groups have a lot of leisure time; neither group is primarily concerned with caring for and feeding children; and both

---

[3] To be fair, Gopnik and Meltzoff sometimes seem to do justice to the distinction between objective and subjective aspects of knowledge. For example, they reject the distinction between context of discovery (subjective) and context of justification (objective) (Gopnik and Meltzoff, 1997, p. 33). But the problem is that they do not maintain and respect this distinction in making specific claims, as I have already indicated. This blurring is especially troublesome when they come to discuss theories and theory change. That is, they present the logical account of theories as though it were a psychological matter (Gopnik and Meltzoff, 1997, p. 34).

groups love truth more than anything else. ('Like scientists, babies sometimes prefer truth to love'; Gopnik and Meltzoff, 1997, p. 152 – said about a child who disobeys its mother.) Further similarities, according to the authors, consist in the fact that both groups of people belong to the same species and have the same type of brain, 'designed' by evolution 'to get things right'. In the end, we seem to be left with the non-controversial and rather trivial claim that there are similarities in cognitive processing in all humans, whether they be children or adults, scientists or people using magic.

RATIONALITY PRESUPPOSED

As I have argued in earlier chapters, one of the most persistent and central problems in developmental psychology is constructing a theory capable of accounting for psychological cognitive change. Different suggestions, like association, deduction, and Piaget's explanatory concepts of assimilation and accommodation, have all run into serious problems. In Chapters 3 and 4, I pointed out the fact that Piaget seems to assume what he sets out to explain, or postulates the same characteristics on another level, mental or biological. Gopnik and Meltzoff's 'theory theory' postulates conceptual or theory change as typical of childhood cognitive development. But this idea makes it necessary to ascribe to children all the properties that we associate with reasonable thinking and rationality. Although the specific contents of the theories change, the basic mechanisms for change remain unchanged, and are presupposed in the explanatory model the authors propose. If children are born with the ability to test, reject, and create theories, there is not really any developmental difference in basic cognitive ability or rationality. In other words, there is no fundamental development and no change over time in the cognitive ability which is shared by all humans. Piaget calls this position intellectual vitalism, alluding to the vitalist explanation of life in terms of a life force (see Piaget, 1936/1963). As we have seen, Gopnik and Meltzoff seem to fall into a similar trap by explaining rationality in terms of rationality. According to their proposal, at best children can be said to change the specific contents of their theories over time, but not their own basic ability to reason.

Even more seriously, these authors confuse knowledge in the objective sense with knowledge in the subjective sense. By transferring the objective conception both of theory and of theory change from science to the subjective or psychological sphere of the child, they have given us not a psychological mechanism, but only a redescription of the way any reasonable person would argue in similar cases. It is just a reconstruction of a rational argument in the objective sense. And by transferring rationality from the public sphere to the private and subjective level, they do not explain the observed level, because the unobserved process is as much in need of explanation as the observed.

Instead of presenting a psychological theory of rationality, then, they postulate an inner, hidden, psychological mechanism mirroring the public discourse we use to describe a rational linguistic discourse.[4] Put another way, they are committing the fallacy of resemblance – i.e., ascribing qualities characteristic of something they are familiar with (as actively working scientists) to that which presumably produces this behaviour, namely psychological mechanisms. This fallacy rests on the assumption that what produces apparently rational behaviour must itself be rational. They (like Piaget) seem to be committing what William James called the 'psychologist's fallacy' of ascribing to their objects of study (infants) characteristics that belong to themselves. As scientists, Gopnik and Meltzoff create, test, and revise theories, so they conclude that children do the same thing. Danziger (1985) points out that Wilhelm Wundt warned against a similar problem, namely the tendency of psychologists to use logic to characterise behaviour, and then illegitimately to transfer this same logical language to the level of psychological mechanisms as well.

---

[4] See Harré (1997); Wittgenstein (1953).

CHILDREN AS PSYCHOLOGISTS: THEORETICIANS
OF THE MIND

The same mistake that underlies Gopnik and Meltzoff's claim also underlies research on children's theories of mind.[5] By seeing children as social scientists or psychologists, these researchers are ascribing to their objects of study (young children) characteristics that belong to themselves. By claiming that children already possess theories and reason, the researchers presuppose what they set out to explain; in this case, social cognition or reasoning.

The claim that children operate with theories of mind in understanding other people is a special case of the more general claim discussed, namely that children are scientists. As I have already noted, detailed and comprehensive discussion of this research literature could easily be the topic of another book. My aim here is only to address the conceptual framework in so far as it, in common with Gopnik and Meltzoff, assumes that children are theoreticians because they test theories in order to discover things about the world as well as about other people, and therefore reason like scientists. According to the 'theory of mind' framework, all of us, including children of three and four years, are assumed to construct 'mental states' like beliefs and desires, and thereby 'explain' and 'predict' behaviour using unobservable theoretical entities which are not publicly available but are inferred from behaviour. Interpersonal understanding and interaction are seen to be based on a theoretical accomplishment involving the individual construction of a theory of one's own as well as others' mental states.

The idea of 'theory of mind' was first introduced by Premack (1976) in his research on the intentionality of primates. Developmental

---

[5] There is a large research literature in this area. For an introduction and overview to the research see for example Martin Doherty's *Theory of Mind: How Children Understand Others' Thoughts and Feelings* (2008), also see Baron-Cohen (1995); Carruthers and Smith (1996). For a critical discussion see Antaki (2004); Costall and Leuder (2004); Reddy and Morris (2004); Shanker (2004); Sharrock and Coulter (2004); Williams (2004); and also Hutto (2008). See Malle (2004) and Malle and Hodges (2005) as well as Erneling (2007, in press) for a discussion of theories of mind more generally.

psychologists studying children's social cognition then adopted this framework, partly as a response to Piaget. In the 1970s a growing body of research showed that children were more competent cognitively and socially than Piaget had claimed (e.g., Donaldson, 1978; for a critical discussion see Costall and Leudar, 2004). This led to a revision of observational data and to certain re-interpretations, but no major or serious theoretical alternative to Piaget and mainstream psychology emerged. Instead it led to a reinforcement of some Cartesian assumptions, by focusing on social cognition as 'mindreading' and its failure as 'mindblindness'.

This approach, like natural learning theories and what I have called mainstream psychology, is profoundly Cartesian; more specifically because it take Descartes' alleged problem of 'other minds' as the starting point. According to Descartes, a person consists of two fundamentally different substances: the mental and the physical. The mental, unlike the physical, does not exist in space, and it is known in a different way. Each of us has privileged access to our own inner, private mental content and structure through introspection, but has to infer the content of other persons' minds, since we only have access to the other person's physical and linguistic behaviour. Speaking and acting are assumed to be public 'representations' of these private cognitive processes and representations, which guide and accompany behaviour that is intentional and rational.

This leads to the problem of understanding other persons. How do we get to know the private, inner, and privileged content of their minds? How do we bridge the gap between the observed behaviour of other people and the hidden content of their minds, their thoughts and feelings? This is roughly how Descartes conceived the problem and it underlies how 'theory of mind' researchers approach children's social abilities. This entails an inherent individualism and internalism, which argue that it is possible to understand other people and their psychology only in terms of what goes on inside their brains, nervous systems, or mental processes, thereby ignoring the individual's relationship to and embodiment in its environment, especially the socio-cultural environment.

This becomes particularly clear in these approaches' metaphor of social cognition as mindreading, which assumes that, like texts, human behaviour needs to be read or interpreted, and inferences made to the meaning of the behaviour, in the form of the mental state 'hidden behind' behaviour. This metaphor clearly highlights the underlying assumption that understanding other people's actions, thoughts, and feelings is a case of inference and interpretation from the observable (behaviour) to something unobserved (mental processes). Thus, proponents of the 'theory of mind' paradigm claim that children as well as ordinary adults are like scientists forming and testing hypotheses, making inferences, constructing theories and the like from the observable (behaviour) to something which cannot be observed (mental processes). Is this a metaphor which helps us to understand social interaction?

In order to be useful, a metaphor or model first has to resemble what it is supposed to illuminate in relevant respects; furthermore it has to be better known than what it is supposed to help us understand and explain. The reading metaphor fails in both aspects, and does not provide an explanation of social cognition.

First, reading a text is vastly more difficult than understanding behaviour including speech in face-to-face situations, the typical contexts in which we are supposed to infer other people's intentions and thoughts. In face-to-face conversations, tone of voice, stress, gestures, and eye contact as well as the social and physical context all help the listener understand how the utterance is to be taken, that is, its illocutionary force (Olson, 1994). Such information – that is, *how* we understand the utterance – is more or less missing in the case of a written text. Texts, with the exception of such marks as '!' and '?', lack information on how the content is to be taken. This led to hermeneutics and other theories of how to interpret texts. There is another difference between reading and understanding others which is related to this.

Unlike understanding others, reading is a skill that does not come naturally from participation in different sociolinguistic contexts, but has to be learned in a systematic way. Therefore there are important differences between reading a text and understanding others. Furthermore, much of our understanding of others seems to be accomplished without constructing theories that contain propositions, as Hutto (2008) points out. According to him, young children, as well as adults, seem to get along without a theory of mind in most everyday encounters and only resort to theories of mind or folk psychological explanations when something goes wrong. 'When things "are as they should be", the narratives of folk psychology are unnecessary' (Bruner, 1990, p. 40). It is interesting to note, as Hutto does, that even Fodor, as a supporter of some central claims of both 'theory theory' and 'theory of mind' approaches, says that folk psychology as a theory of mind 'works so well it disappears' (Fodor, 1987, p. 3). Thus, it seems that 'mind-reading' is only taking place when something goes wrong, and is not the typical way of making sense of others. In this context, Hutto's distinction between propositional attitudes, which are required for 'mindreading', and intentional attitudes, which do not entail propositions or a theoretical approach, is well worth a hearing (Hutto, 2008).

Second, psychologists' understanding and explanations of what goes on in the case of reading are no better than their understanding of social interaction in face-to-face situations; on the contrary, there seems to be more scientific knowledge about how children come, for example, to grasp the fact that other people have feelings, thoughts, and beliefs than there is about the process involved in learning to read.

More fundamentally, the reading metaphor is based on a dubious conception of mental activity. As already mentioned, mainstream developmental psychology uncritically adopts an approach to mental life which presupposes individualism and internalism. In this approach, the task of the psychologist is to infer, describe, and if possible explain these hidden, inner mental processes of ordinary people. This is similar to the task the 'theory of mind' researchers assume all of us, including infants, face every day – inferring hidden mental processes on the basis of external behaviour. As we saw in the case of Gopnik and Meltzoff, psychology researchers transfer their approach to understanding others from the context of the research laboratory to everyday situations, committing the fallacy of resemblance mentioned above.

This conception of mind is problematic because it focuses on how humans function solely in terms of what goes on in their brains, nervous systems, or minds, disregarding their constant and dynamic entanglement with the environment, especially the socio-cultural environment. Mental activity is not only what goes on inside our heads disconnected from the world around us. Our brain and mental processes depend on the environment both for their development and for their function, because it scaffolds, as it were, our interactions. This is important not only because people internalise some of this in the process of becoming socialised, but also because it is the external framework that sets the stage for acts and provides clues of how an action should be taken, that is, its illocutionary force. Meaningfulness and intentionally are not only in people's minds (or brains), but also distributed in the linguistic and non-linguistic social field of interaction itself. Theories of mind or folk psychology are an important aspect of this environment, but have their basis in public social practices. Folk psychological narratives, for example fairy tales and children's books, help children construct their folk psychological theories (see Hutto, 2008).

To reduce social understanding to internal individual processes therefore misses something crucial. It is like conceiving of a game of tennis as a competitive game 'explained by reference to the physics of elastic impacts and ballistic trajectories' (see Harré, 2000, p. 4). In order to understand, explain, and sometimes predict what is taking place on centre court, we also need the rules of tennis. And the same goes for our understanding of others generally. Our ability in everyday situations to describe someone as angry or making a promise is not typically based on inferences about their mental or brain processes but involves the socio-cultural framework. This is one reason why folk psychology theories or narratives seem to disappear in everyday life, as Fodor (1987) points out. They are not needed because there is already enough information in the external social context, in the social practices, and in the roles, rules, and rituals which Erwing Goffman (e.g., 1974) in particular has explored with his dramaturgical model, one which has been developed further by, for example, positioning theory (Harré and Moghaddam, 2003).

Thus it is not surprising that nurses are good at giving the surgeon the correct instruments during surgery. There is external scaffolding in the physical situation of the operating theatre, in the social expectations, and in the rules of the specific type of surgery to be performed, as well as in the different prescribed roles of the participants. If the social scaffolding or framework is absent or if someone behaves 'out of character', the situation becomes different and difficult indeed; we would then have a hard time and might start guessing what is going on in other people's minds. Experimental situations in the psychological laboratory are often like this: situations where the normal social framework is missing or presented in an artificial way. In this case, the normal dynamics enabling smooth interaction and social competence will be missing as well. So it should not surprise us either that adults and young children in such situations do not perform very well or that when they do it seems such a mystery; neither should it surprise us that psychologists miss the importance of the socio-cultural scaffolding. And it is the same with reading. As Olson says, 'To be literate it is not enough to know the words; one must learn how to participate in the discourse of some textual community' (Olson, 1994, p. 273). Once again, to explain typically human mental phenomena only in terms of what is inside the skull is like trying to explain tennis as a competitive game by referring only to the physics of ballistic trajectories. It is by ignoring this framework and by reducing social competence and performance to individual and inner processes that social understanding and competence are made to appear so mysterious and difficult to make sense of.

By pointing to the importance of socio-cultural frameworks I do not mean to deny the fact that social competence and performance require a normally functioning brain, or to say that recent research on mirror neurons does not throw light on the issue (see for example Arbib, 2005; Rizzolatti, Fogassi, and Gallese, 2001). The activation of motor neurons in the brain of a primate or person observing another primate or person raising an arm clearly seems to help in understanding what is going on, but the activation itself cannot specify whether the raised arm is a greeting or a threat. This is to be found only in the specific context and the socio-cultural milieu in which it is embedded. What I am proposing is that we get rid of the reductionist Cartesian approach to understanding the mental; namely that reductionism which assumes that mental capacities are essentially individual internal capacities.[6]

CONCLUSION: COGNITION AND MIND

I strongly endorse theoretical developments in psychology, of which there are far too few, in comparison with empirical work. With this in mind, we can say that Piaget, Gopnik and Meltzoff, and other theorists in developmental psychology are attempting to do the right thing. Yet in spite of all their theoretical assumptions and empirical results, the fundamental problems of cognitive change, learning, and the nature of rationality remain.

The reason for this, as I have already indicated, is that they are still too much part of the mainstream Cartesian–Kantian 'ideal of psychological order', which (1) often confuses the objective with the subjective sense of knowledge and belief, and (2) as a consequence of this does not distinguish clearly between what one could call cognition on the one side and the mind on the other (see van Gelder, 2005). Hutto, in critically discussing the 'theory of mind' literature, suggests that we should make a distinction between intentional attitudes not involving propositions and propositional attitudes. The former are present to

---

[6] The same reductionism of mental activity is found in evolutionary psychology, and in addition to other problems (see for example Munz, 2004), its explanations fail because they overlook the social-external and situated aspects of mental activity. Thus evolutionary psychology is as much a part of mainstream psychology as the approaches discussed in this chapter. Even if their approach to evolution is an improvement on Piaget in several aspects, they have in common many problematic assumptions.

different degrees in non-human animals, infants, and also adults and are the basis for children learning folk psychology theories or narratives (Hutto, 2008). Propositional attitudes require a language and are in this sense tied to public and social practices. I think that here Hutto is trying to make a similar point to van Gelder, namely that not everything that we think of as mental activity involves the same processes.

By cognition I mean all the states and processes which form the causal underpinnings of all our sophisticated behaviour, from wine tasting to playing football and doing mathematics. The most complex component in cognition is the brain; but our body considered more generally is also important. Cognition is individual, and mostly inside the skin or skull, but it also involves skills and behaviours of different kinds. It is a physical process and involves causal mechanisms. There is no mystery about the ontological status of cognition seen in this way. Cognition is simply a physical, biological process, involving different behavioural skills (see Chapter 6 and Erneling, 1993).

But the mind also includes beliefs and knowledge, which involve something else besides the physical or biological processes or mechanisms of an individual – namely norms and social institutions. For example, think about what kind of physical structure we would call a church: there is the actual physical building, which is quite complex; but for it to be a church, there has to be agreement among the members of the community to call and use it as a church, and for this to be possible there have to be certain norms and social institutions in place. In a similar way, scientific activity is more than the cognition of scientists. Likewise, being an individual who believes is more than having cognition; it is also participating in a specific social and linguistic setting according to certain norms. Acts of anger or linguistic or cognitive competence are individuated not just by being associated with particular neurological cognitive events, but by being acts or activities that take place 'at' some specific person, who is part of a group of people within which interaction with each other is made sense of through rules. Making a promise or being angry involves a functioning brain and mental processes, but it also involves having other people consider the public utterance or behaviour to be a promise or anger, as well as the appropriate external context. If I promise you something verbally, it does not matter what specific state my brain is in. Rather, the important thing is that my promise is taken as such by other people, and that the situation is such that it gives me the right to make a promise. And this depends not just on my and your behaviour and presumed mental processes, but also on a social network of meanings and rules. Or think about anger: no matter what goes on in my brain, or in my thinking or behaviour, if what I say or scream is not taken as anger by the people around me in the specific context, but is seen as an instance of madness or acting, the reference to mental processes is meaningless.

Consider further a short illustration from language acquisition. One, obviously too simple, way to decompose linguistic competence is to say that it involves the acquisition of speech perception skills, speech production skills, syntactical skills, and semantically communicative skills. This is enough for the point I want to make here, since I shall elaborate on it in the next chapter. Undoubtedly, the acquisition of all such skills presupposes a functioning brain and other physiological and cognitive functions. And this fact needs to be studied. But to explain what happens here, we also need to look beyond it. To learn to utter something meaningful – that is, to acquire semantically communicative skills – is not just to acquire the specific configuration of brain or other physical processes or behaviours. It also involves having other people consider what one says to be a piece of linguistic communication. For the third time, to explain typically human mental phenomena only in terms of the brain and/or cognition is like trying to explain tennis as a competitive game by referring to the physics of ballistic trajectories.

Thus, in order to understand cognitive development (which even in its name is misleading), we need to study both these aspects and see how they interact, and not confuse them by trying to reduce one to the other. Mentality involving cognition is something which combines brain and culture, but the issue of how this is done still is unresolved in the 'theory theory' and 'theory of mind' approaches, as it is in Piaget and the natural learning theories inspired by Piaget's constructivism. This failure is to a large extent due to the individualism and biologism of the mainstream 'ideal of psychological order' approach. In the next chapter I want to propose an alternative to this.

6 The socio-cultural approach to learning

In previous chapters, and especially in Chapter 1, I claimed that there is a tendency towards the infantilisation of education. This is especially prevalent in the literature on the educational use of computer technologies. The ideas and arguments presented in this literature to a large extent rely on what can be called natural learning theories, which in general see learning as a natural process like the acquisition of one's first language and basic concepts and skills during infancy. Computer technology, according to this approach, helps schools create situations in which children learn everything in the same enjoyable and easy way they acquired basic cognitive skills in infancy, the paradigm of natural learning. One could also describe this as the infantilisation of science, since more recent theoretical approaches, represented by those of 'theory theory' and 'theory of mind', claim that infants and scientists reason in a similar way. It is these natural learning theories that I have discussed critically above. In this chapter, I shall present an alternative approach to learning, which instead sees socio-cultural activities, rather than natural individual reactions, as paradigmatic.

Natural learning theories go back a long time and include, most prominently, those of Jean-Jacques Rousseau, but their modern form, as we noted above, is inspired particularly by Piaget and his followers. In addition to these, there are Chomsky's ideas of an innate universal grammar and language acquisition as hypothesis testing, as well as other versions of internalist constructivist theories that have been influential. These theories are, as I have argued in previous chapters, all part of mainstream individualistic and mentalistic psychology, which in its turn has grown out of the Cartesian–Kantian philosophy of mind and knowledge. The central assumption of this 'ideal of psychological order' is that perception, memory, learning, cognition, etc. are to be explained in terms of underlying, conscious and unconscious mental states and processes of individuals. As noted earlier, the key attributes of mental states are intentionality and normativity. Just to reiterate briefly: intentionality refers to the fact that mental processes and states have meaning for the person who has them.[1] They are states that are experienced as being directed at something other than themselves. When we think about an angel, or see a dog, or believe it is going to rain tomorrow, the content of our thoughts is about something other than the thoughts themselves, namely the angel, the dog, and the rain. Thoughts point beyond themselves in providing representations of something, and in that they are meaningful to the person having them. In this sense, mental activity always involves symbols, that is, meaningful representations. A state or process is normative if it is routinely subject to the possibility of being evaluated according to standards or norms of correctness. In these aspects, namely those concerning their normativity and intentionality, mental states and processes are different from other phenomena studied by science. Yet mainstream psychology tries to reduce explanations of the normativity and intentionality of mental activity to explanations based on physics, neurophysiology, or biology.

Piaget, as noted, takes these aspects of mental states and cognition seriously in his account of cognitive development and learning. He thinks that the normativity of mental states is something constructed in the process of their development as mental states, and claims that their content becomes more equilibrated and thereby more objective, certain, etc. Intentionality is characteristic of mental operations acquired by children through the early skills of imitation and symbolic play. As I have shown above, he tries to connect these typical and unique aspects of mental states and processes to biological foundations, or more specifically tries to explain them in terms of functional invariants or laws of development, shared by all organisms.

[1] For a discussion of these and related issues see Harré (2001).

In common with mainstream psychology, Piaget searches for universal processing mechanisms or psychological laws, in his case the laws of evolutionary progress, based on observed behaviours and patterns of thought in children. According to the mainstream 'ideal of psychological order', such universal processing mechanisms (like hypothesis testing) operate independently of culture, context, task, and stimulus content. In this belief in the independence of culture and specific context, 'theory theory' and 'theory of mind' approaches are included and are similar to Piaget's universal functional invariants of biology.

Piaget fails to resolve the problems of learning – the productivity and the framework – because, although critical of some aspects of it, he accepts the mainstream approach which sees both productivity and the framework as functions grounded in individual mental activity, which in its turn is explained by the underlying psychological and biological laws. He is therefore seeking nothing less than the reconciliation of norms and meaning (culture/convention) with biology (nature). In the end, however, he reduces them to universal biological laws, making the individual human being as a learner the passive 'vessel' for these universal laws or biological processing mechanisms, ones which function independently of specific stimulus content and varying contexts.[2] Nevertheless, his focus on the central aspects of mentality, intentionality, and normativity, as well as certain of his more specific ideas (imitation and symbolic play for example), are valuable and can be utilised in a context which does not reduce mental activity to biology. He is also correct to stress the fact that human beings are active and are constantly confronting change, since no experience is like any other, and to criticise rationalism and empiricism for their view of knowledge and its development. These elements of his views are utilised below in order to develop an alternative, discursive account of cognitive development and learning.

---

[2] The same is true of contemporary evolutionary psychology. See for example Munz (2004), who argues that the mind in evolutionary psychology is seen as a bucket into which the environment pours information via the senses, which are adapted to pick out the relevant information, while the individual remains passive.

The theory of learning proposed by natural learning theories, including Piaget's, is thus problematic, and more specifically fails to account for both the framework and productivity, as I argued in Chapters 3 and 4. These approaches fail because of their mistaken account of the key attributes of mental activity: normativity and intentionality. Neither the necessary framework for learning nor productivity can be reduced to inner, private, and subjective states or processes of the individual. Instead, the framework and productivity should be accounted for by individual physiological abilities and bodily skills *and* by the normative and meaningful structures provided in social interactions and the cognitive artefacts associated with them. Psychological activity is distributed through such interactions as the conversations in which memories are constructed or decisions reached.

Furthermore, natural learning theories presuppose what they intend to explain by postulating rationality and cognition on a different level, one hidden behind observed behaviours. This move lacks explanatory value, as Wittgenstein has shown (1953), because postulating a similar mechanism at a hidden, less well-understood mental level does not provide its own explanation. A process of regression therefore begins. In addition, by theorising an inner, unobserved level, which in most cases is of necessity also unobservable and thus not conscious to the person having the state in question, this move makes the state lose the characteristic of a mental state altogether, and therefore become not intentional or meaningful for the person having it.[3]

All mental activity is fundamentally in flux and is always productive, as Piaget recognises, but this flux or productivity is not ordered by individual judgements or biological laws, but by the external socio-cultural environment and cognitive artefacts such as language, scientific theories and practices, etc. These provide meaning and norms.

Human beings are biological beings and our bodies and brains are enabling conditions for mental activity and development, but they are

---

[3] For a discussion of this see Harré (2001); Searle (1983).

not all there is to cognition, development, and learning. Psychologists often mistakenly try to reduce mental activity to enabling conditions, as for instance Gopnik and Meltzoff do when they try to compare children's cognitive development to scientific change, another Piagetian idea. The cognitive skills of scientists are enabling conditions for science, but the conditions of scientific change are not a function of the laws of the physiology of individual brains or private cognitive activities. As I claimed in Chapter 5, seeing science and cognitive development in infants as Gopnik and Meltzoff do is a little like trying to reduce a game of tennis to the physics of rackets, nets, balls, and human brains and limbs.[4] All these are clearly enabling conditions for the game, but the rules of a game of tennis are not the laws of physics or human physiology. The rules or norms of tennis are jointly worked out, negotiated, and followed by the people playing and watching tennis. In an analogous way, the human body and its brain are enabling conditions for cognition, but the norms of correctness and rules of meaning are not the regularities or laws of physics or of neurophysiology. The norms of correctness and meaning are found in social interactions involving cultural practices and artefacts, and they shape the use of the body etc. to accomplish tasks like playing a game of tennis, participating in a conversation, or learning a new skill such as reading. The norms and rules are, at least initially, external to the individual and shape the individual's activity. They are sometimes explicitly formulated, as in cases of rule following when one is using an explicated, formulated rule to guide one's use of words and behaviour. Sometimes, too, acting in accordance with the rules is a metaphor for acting in an orderly way because one has acquired a habit, or carries on a well-established practice.

Furthermore, natural learning theories' focus on the individual and his or her biological and innate capabilities reduces learning to the learning of biologically primary cognitive skills (see Chapter 1). But both early and later learning involve the application of varied

---

[4] The analogy of tennis is from Harré (2001).

socio-cultural norms and contexts that give meaning to and set standards for what is learned. Learning and cognitive development as a whole are always a discursive and socio-cultural activity, even in the very first and early activities of infancy, for example the acquisition of one's mother tongue.

This alternative 'ideal of psychological order' assumes that the discursive process of cognition is found as much in public and collective activity as in individual natural abilities and skills. It thus rejects the individualistic account of the framework and of productivity. This, as I shall show in more detail below, has consequences for the account of learning.

THE ACQUISITION OF LANGUAGE: THE DOMESTICATION OF NATURAL SKILLS

Introduction: The internal and external aspects of the framework

There are several reasons why it is fruitful to focus this discussion of an alternative approach to learning and mental activity on the acquisition of language. As we have seen in Chapter 2, the paradigm for learning put forth by theorists of natural learning is the acquisition of one's first language. Not surprisingly, they claim to be interested in studying the learning of language because it is the most characteristic of human cognitive achievements, and it is the basic symbol-utilising skill that is presupposed in all higher mental functioning. Accounting for intentionality and normativity therefore cannot be avoided. The reader is asked to follow this detour as a means of getting a better understanding of learning more generally. I will return to this topic in Chapter 7.

In this section, I shall show how language acquisition, although involving many natural, biological, and innate skills as enabling conditions, is nevertheless a cultural achievement. It is more like what mainstream psychology sees as secondary cognitive skills. This process, I argue, can fruitfully, be characterised as a 'domestication' of the unfolding, natural, innate abilities of the infant. One learns a language by being domesticated, that is, by having one's natural reactions and behaviours shaped in accordance with prevailing semantic-communicative activities of one's family environment.[5]

The two main problems any theory of learning has to solve also occur in the case of explaining language acquisition. The problem of productivity involves, as Chomsky (1959) points out, the fact that any competent language user can understand and produce a potentially infinite number of sentences. The problem of the framework has to do with the seemingly logical requirement that learning a language requires already knowing a language, that is, one already has to have a framework of meaning and linguistic norms.

Coming to be a competent user of a language does not and could not occur in an isolated individual (see for example the discussion of Piaget's account of meaning in Chapter 4). Acquiring one's first language is not a solitary achievement of an individual exploiting his or her innate, natural abilities or basic mental framework, one containing both inherent meaning and a mechanism for productivity. It is a joint activity involving the child, its caregivers, and the surrounding language and language community. Piaget was right in claiming that all mental activity is productive in the sense that it is constantly changing and that in order to explain cognitive development, or, in the case under consideration, language acquisition, one should not focus on this 'natural' productivity or flux. Instead, the problem is how this natural flux, or going beyond the information given, gets formed in accordance with prevailing norms. While it is true that any competent language user can produce a potentially infinite set of sentences, they have all to be in accordance with rules of grammar or pragmatics to count as sentences. Not any combination of speech sounds or words count as productive use. Neither the individual child nor the caregiver can by himself or herself provide the necessary framework for learning. To speak meaningfully is not only to perceive or utter speech sounds idiosyncratically, but also to do it correctly

---

[5] See Hutto (2008) for a discussion of the importance of language for the acquisition of theories of mind and folk psychology.

according to the implicit or explicit rules of the surrounding language community. This assumes that the framework necessary for language acquisition consists of three interacting frameworks, of which all are productive: the innate biological skills of the individual; the social, mostly face-to-face, contexts within which language is used; and finally, language itself.

I have chosen to call the theory of language acquisition which I describe below the *domestication model*[6] to stress that language learning is not natural learning but a matter of social training, in which the infant's natural behaviours and reactions are shaped by sociolinguistic interactions. The framework for learning consists not of innate or individually acquired cognitive-mental structures, but of a combination of the child's natural endowments and behaviours, sociolinguistic interactions, and the language spoken in the surroundings. The child's pre-language behaviour is constantly changing due to maturation, changing bodily activities, and experiences, and it is through training in a social context that this productivity is distinguished from mere randomness, thereby making way for meaningful language and communication. To show this, one does not need to undertake new empirical studies, but to use what is already known about children and interpret it in a new way, from a non-individualistic and non-mentalistic perspective.

Infants' brains, their perception and production of speech sounds, increasingly complex motor behaviour, and activities like imitation and play, all change as a result of maturation and sociolinguistic interactions and training. Around the child's first birthday, they all come together, resulting in the first display of language skills. It is at this time that the child's more-or-less indiscriminate babbling has narrowed and shaped into words of the infant's mother tongue. This is accomplished by the coming together of the individual internal and external natural framework and social interactions embedded in the external language community.

---

[6] For a more detailed discussion of this model see Erneling (1993).

It is thus fruitful to look at language acquisition as the socio-cultural assembling and modifying of two different sets of skills, which become interrelated, with one overruling the other. Both skills have their origin in individual motor behaviours. Learning a language involves a purely linguistic aspect, phonemic and syntactical skills – the perception and production of speech sounds in accordance with syntactical rules – and a communicative-semantic aspect – the communication of concepts in different circumstances with different people. A precondition for this is the plasticity and redundancy of the developing brain (see for example Changeux, 1985; Elman *et al.*, 1996; Wexler, 2006).

The behaviours and skills involved in the phonemic and syntactic aspects of language are present early in the infant's life, some even from birth, e.g., the capacity to discriminate speech sounds. Others, like the ability to utter speech sounds, come into play when the relevant anatomical structures (e.g., the voice box) have developed, but cannot be successfully used for anything resembling language until the communicative and semantic skills have become complex enough. This, as mentioned, occurs around the infant's first birthday. At this time, the phonemic and linguistic skills have been shaped and changed by the sociolinguistic environment, that is, by conversations with competent language users who function as models to imitate, but even more importantly as interlocutors that shape the infant's use of his or her skills. In this way the infant is learning the explicit and implicit conventions and norms. At an early stage, this is done by what I call symbiosis, which I explain in more detail later. In symbiotic interaction, the adult encourages and discourages the infant not only on the basis of behaviours, but also on the basis of attributed semantic and communicative intent, which the adult reads into the behaviours. In this way, adults initially 'speak for the child' in conversations involving the two of them. Thus, as the child is treated as being in a position to mean things, to 'intend' to communicate and so on, its purely natural behaviours (e.g., phonemic and syntactical) are brought into line with and take on meaning and communicative intent. This is the beginning of language acquisition and also of acquiring the first meaningful and normative framework, on which later cognitive development rests.

Although language is found only in humans, rudiments of relevant skills are found in non-human primates. These latter can be taught to use signs for simple descriptions and requests which resemble those of a two- to three-year-old child, but do not develop their language-like skills any further (see for example Erneling, 1993; Shanker and Taylor, 2005; Tomasello, 2000). This shows that, although language is species-specific, some of the skills involved are not, but are present to some degree in other species as well. What are unique to humans are some specific skills like speech production and a socio-cultural niche which includes linguistic and other normative practices. This shaping of natural behaviours and reactions by the socio-cultural environment takes advantage of the slowly developing human brain. Once language has developed, it enhances different natural skills, leading to further differences from other species.

In sum: in language acquisition, natural behaviours and reactions are utilised and shaped in close interpersonal contexts as well as in the community-wide environment, which uses language according to certain conventions and norms. Language acquisition is based on an individual as well as a public collective framework. The individual part of the framework consists of phonemic and syntactical skills as well as skills like imitation and symbolic play and also natural reactions involved in social interactions. The collective part is made up of social interactions and symbiosis as well as public collective norms explicit or implicit in actual language use. Let me now explore and support this account in more detail.

Phonemic and syntactic skills: the individual framework
As already noted, the human infant is equipped with special anatomical and neural mechanisms for the basic phonemic aspects of language and the perception and production of speech sounds. Newborn infants sense the loudness and pitch of speech sounds as well as adults do

(Bijeljac-Babic, Bertocini, and Mehler, 1993; Juszcyk and Derrah, 1987; Juszcyk *et al.*, 1993; Sinnott, Pison, and Askin, 1983), and after a few weeks the infant detects discrete phonemes as well (Eimas, 1985; see also De Boysson-Bardies *et al.*, 1993; MacNeilage, 2008; Menn and Stoel-Gammon, 1993). These early perceptual skills do not seem to be learned and are sometimes better than adults' abilities. But they are increasingly changed and limited by the language activities in which the infant takes part. Infants soon acquire the ability to recognise the specific speech sounds of the language spoken around them, but lose the abilities to discriminate others. For example, seven-month-old infants from an English-speaking environment, but not those twelve months old, can detect certain sounds of Hindi (Eimas, 1985; Juszcyk *et al.*, 1993; MacNeilage, 2008; Werker and Tees, 1984).[7]

The ability to perceive speech sounds is not unique to humans (Walker, 1987), but the ability to produce speech sounds seems to be. As the human voice box matures around three months of age, the first speech-like sounds such as cooing start to occur. Around six months, babbling follows this accomplishment. Up until their first birthday all infants, including deaf children, incorporate virtually all sounds of human language into their babbling (see for example Kimbrough Oller, 2000; MacNeilage, 2008; Menn and Stoel-Gammon, 1993). As in the case of speech perception, speech production seems to be genetically coded, and is also greatly modified by experience and the activity of the language spoken around the child (see for example De Boysson-Bardies *et al.*, 1993). Thus, infants eventually come to produce a narrower range of speech sounds or phonemes, namely the ones used in their native language.

In order to use these modified phonemic skills in any form resembling language, the child has to use them in a systematic and normative way corresponding to their use in the mother tongue. This means that they have to be used in a grammatically or syntactically

---

[7] For a discussion of early speech perception and production see also Gervain and Werker (2008); Kuhl (2004).

correct way. If Chomsky is correct, these syntactical skills also have an innate basis, but the forms that the child actually comes to use are the result of linguistic encounters with its native language. It is also worth mentioning that children early on engage in much non-linguistic behaviour that is in accordance with rules. Lieberman (1984, 1985; Lieberman and Blumstein, 1988; see also MacNeilage, 2008 for a discussion of speech and motor behaviour) and Sinclair (1971) suggest that syntactical skills are based on utilising non-linguistic behaviours in a linguistic context. Whether or not syntactic skills build on specific, innate linguistic models or on more general abilities, they seem to be grounded in human biology.

In sum: the claim is that the phonemic as well as syntactical skills, both of which are necessary for language but not sufficient, are partly the result of an individual framework which contains speech production and perceptual skills as well as syntactic-like skills. But this development also requires active participation in a linguistic community, that is, an external framework that not only provides models for speech, but also involves the child in linguistic interactions in different contexts.

Semantic skills: the public, shared framework

There is more to language than uttering phonemes in accordance with syntactical rules: even if a parrot utters a complete sentence, this does not mean that it is speaking a language. One also has to say something meaningful that one understands, and one has to produce these sounds in varying contexts and to different people. Thus language requires semantic and communicative-interactive skills as well. In other words, the child has to acquire intentionality and norms. The child has to be able to re-present and use sounds in accordance with the norms of the surrounding linguistic society.

Speaking meaningfully, that is, acquiring semantic skills, involves two different aspects, as Piaget claimed (see Chapter 4 above). First, the child has to master the ability to use one thing – an object or linguistic or other sign – to stand for and represent something else. Second, the child has to acquire and understand the meaning of words and other linguistic symbols of his or her language. The first type of ability or skill is, as we have seen in Chapter 4, based on two more rudimentary skills which have an innate basis but develop during the first year, namely imitation and symbolic play.

According to Piaget (1945/1962), infants begin to imitate quite early during their first year. But it is later, between eighteen and twenty-four months, that they become capable of deferred imitation. The infant is now able to imitate complex new models, objects as well as persons, whether present or absent. This means that behaviours can be taken out of their immediate contexts and exhibited in novel situations. In a sense, the infant can use behaviours productively because he or she can relate them to other, different contexts, situations, or objects. This displacement is the beginning of symbolic play and, more significantly, of semantic skills. Behavioural patterns, first externalised and later internalised, that are associated with one context can now stand for it in another context. Before the age of twenty-four months, the infant normally has acquired 50 words, but around this age the vocabulary begins to grow to around 200 words.

In sum: mastering the skill of imitation and also of symbolic play has enabled the infant both to 'tailor' its speech sounds, through practice, to the sound pattern occurring in its sociolinguistic environment, and to master the skill of letting behaviours stand for or signal something else.

The second type of skill, that is, using words in a meaningful way, is the result of combining imitation and symbolic play with the child's growing social skills, ones which have developed in the proximate and normative interactions with others. Social-communicative interaction is important because it delimits idiosyncratic symbols or meanings, and constrains the productivity inherent in the child's early activities. Without this delimitation there would be no meaning, even for individual infants. This is the case because an idiosyncratic and private symbol is not a symbol in the sense that it has stable meaning for the child. As I showed in Chapter 4, private images or intention to mean the same thing are not enough for meaningful symbols. These are fixed only in social interactions. Social interaction therefore provides the context of meaning which connects the child's individual activities with a public language having shared conventional meanings. The skills of representation and of meaning come together as a package, not one after the other, as Piaget assumed.

Communicative-social skills: the public, shared framework
To have a language-using capacity is not only to be able to speak in well-formed sentences or to be able to use words with idiosyncratic meanings, but to be able to meet the requirements of the sociolinguistic environment. The infant has somehow got to acquire signs and symbols that are fixed enough to allow communication and information gathering, but are general enough to 'embody' experiences that go beyond individual experiences. The infant has to learn to mean the same thing with its words and sentences as the rest of the sociolinguistic community does, which is to say that it must acquire a communicative and social skill. One must be able to adjust what one is saying to the person to whom one is speaking, to speak with a purpose, to say relevant things and be sensitive to the discursive context. The social and communicative skills build on the skills I have discussed above, but also on some very specific and pre-linguistic social skills. It is when theses skills are combined or converge around the infant's first birthday that we finally have the beginning of language capability.[8]

Before turning to the specific social skills involved in language acquisition, something has to be said about the character of the linguistic input the infant encounters. Considered as a database for making generalisations about the syntactic, semantic, and pragmatic rules involved in language use, the input is incomplete and underdetermines what can be learned. According to the discursive or domestication

---

[8] For a discussion of the importance of social interaction and cultural practices see for example Baldwin (2000); Blaffer Hrdy (2009); Rogoff (1990); Tomasello (1999, 2000).

model, the infant cannot utilise these data without the help of the structuring which the sociolinguistic environment provides. The infant's ability to engage in social interaction is necessary not only to acquire the conventional skills in language use, but also to make sense of the input.

Let me explain. Chomsky (1959) points out in his criticism of Skinner that the language the infant hears is incomplete and faulty as a database, a fact which is apparent from listening to any normal conversation in a family. But the situation is worse in the sense that the infant encounters only a limited set of examples of any particular language usage. Add to this the indeterminacy of all use of language and the task of learning seems impossible. If language and thought are inherently underdetermined or open-ended, that is, if any lexical item can be used in an indefinite number of ways, just overhearing examples (often faulty) of speech cannot by itself be the ground from which the infant acquires its language. This is what has led Chomsky and others to preformism or the idea of innate linguistic and cognitive structures, that is, an internal, individual framework. But an alternative is possible, if one assumes that the structuring and limiting framework is found in the infant's social interactions, and is thus external to the infant. We do not need to assume an innate language of thought or an acquired internal meaningful discourse (as Piaget does) in order to explain how the infant learns from experience and becomes competent in normative linguistic usage. Furthermore, the learning mechanism involved is neither a language acquisition device (LAD), nor a universal evolutionary law or induction or deduction, but a process of training or the domestication of non-social and non-normative skills in accordance with local norms and standards.

In sum: social interaction and the acquisition of social skills have two functions: they help the infant to utilise and learn from experience and to acquire the conventions of language. What the infant's own mind is not providing is provided by interactions with adults. Thus the infant's natural behaviour is shaped according to the standards and norms of the sociolinguistic environment.

Symbiosis

The learning of language resembles the training of animals: just as the trainer of a circus animal or a dog rearranges, recombines, and shapes innate and natural behaviours according to some external norms, the sociolinguistic environment domesticates the infant to become a speaker. The infant's innate motor behaviours and reactions (phonemic and syntactical skills, object manipulation, imitation, play, etc.) are combined to meet the standards of the sociolinguistic community. This process can be understood in terms of symbiosis (see for example Blaffer Hrdy, 2009; Erneling, 1993; Shotter, 1974, 1976).

By symbiosis I mean a relationship in which the infant is dependent on the adult not only for the satisfaction of its physical needs, but also for social, linguistic, and mental activity. Not only does the adult provide instances of use, in for example baby talk, and by correcting the infant's own attempts to speak; adults engage in conversations with infants. This is done in such a way as to ascribe to the infant meanings and thoughts that the infant would have uttered if he or she had been a fully developed member of the linguistic community. These supplementations are based on the infant's natural expressions and behaviours and, later on, its limited repertoire of linguistic utterances. Parents speak for infants, as in 'Is baby tired?', 'Oh, we're so tired', 'Does baby want to go sleepies?', 'We want to take our nap now, don't we?', and so on. Parents thus pretend to have a two-way conversation with the infant (see for example Hoff-Ginsberg, 1997, chs 5 and 6; Sachs, 1993). In this way, parents seem to be trying to help infants express themselves by offering supplements to what infants currently provide for themselves. These offerings come to serve as models for later usage.

Furthermore, the parent or caregiving adult not only ascribes meanings and thoughts to the infant, but also reacts to the infant as if he or she had actually thought or meant something specific. The adult treats the infant as a (mental) unity, but this unity is symbiotic, since it consists of the infant's actual behaviours together with the interpretation and supplementation the adult gives to the infant's behaviour. In this way, the infant's expressions of innately based, idiosyncratic speech-sound productions are incorporated into a social and communicative context. The infant becomes a rational being by being treated as a rational being.

The symbiotic dyad of the mother (or other caregiver) and the infant can be viewed as one psychological or linguistic being, where the mother gives social, intersubjective, or conventional meaning to what the infant does naturally and instinctively without concern for others. The mother, by interpreting the infant's behaviour and reactions and then acting on them accordingly, co-ordinates her own behaviour with the infant's. From the very start, the infant's reactions and behaviours are part of a social system, one which is both more stable and more extensive than the infant's individual reactions. In the beginning, the infant does not make a distinction between its own and the mother's actions (Piaget, 1937/1954), but sees them as a continuation of its own behaviour. The interaction is one-sided and not really social in that the infant is not an actor but a recipient. As the infant grows and acquires skills such as manipulating objects, true imitation, and so on, he or she starts to play an active role, performing those meaningful actions himself or herself, eventually making the supplementation by the mother superfluous. Around fifteen months the infant begins to say 'No!' to the mother and is able to resist the mother's interpretations of its behaviour, wishes, etc. (see Shotter, 1976). The symbiotic relationship is breaking and the infant is becoming a social actor in his or her own right.[9]

The symbiosis has trained the infant first by combining his or her actions with another's, then by co-ordinating the infant's behaviour with that of others in a patterned and reciprocal way, and eventually, in social play, by doing this in accordance with shared conventional norms. By participating in forms of life, the infant becomes prepared

---

[9] See also Rogoff (1990, 2003) for a discussion of early proto-social interactions; Hutto (2008) for a discussion of early, pre-verbal intentional attitudes

to participate in language games and to acquire the management of the meaning, syntax, and pragmatics of the language spoken around it.

The infant is pre-adapted for symbiosis and social interaction (Blaffer Hrdy, 2009; Rogoff, 1990, 2003; Tomasello, 1999, 2008) by such automatic responses as reflexive crying, smiling, and selective attention to speech sounds and human faces. Much of the infant's early reflexive behaviour is patterned, which enables the mother to relate her own actions in a systematic way to the infant's, for example by smiling and talking to the infant only in pauses between suckling. There is evidence that these early interactions are patterned and stereotyped in most mother–infant dyads (Blaffer Hrdy, 2009; Bower, 1977; Richards, 1974; Rogoff, 1990), but it should be noted that although the infant's behaviour is innate and reflexive, the mother's interpretations (and subsequent reaction) involve cultural assumptions. There is no predetermined labelling of universal behaviours. In Western cultures, crying is often seen as a sign of hunger, but for mothers among !Kung-speaking Bushmen, where the infant is carried on the mother's back most of the time, certain movements are taken to be the usual signs for hunger (Konner, 1972). The same is illustrated by the 'Baby X' experiments. In these experiments, adults are shown infants labelled as girls or boys and the adult is asked to describe the behaviour of the infant (for example, reaction to a the sudden appearance of a Jack–in–the-box doll). If the adult thinks the child is a girl, it is described as reacting and feeling different things (e.g., fear) from those described if the adult thinks the infant is a boy (e.g., anger).[10]

But the ascription of meanings to different behaviours cannot be completely arbitrary, because the infant would never be satisfied or might not even survive (see also Blaffer Hrdy, 2009; Gray, 1978; Lock, 1978). However, there seems to be enough variation and diversity of natural expression to allow for enormous cultural and contextual variation. Hence, infants' behaviours are from the beginning combined and co-ordinated with those of others on the basis of social norms. The

---

[10] See for example Vasta *et al.* (1999).

very meaning and significance of the infant's reactions are thus restricted by social norms, and so are the stimuli and input, both linguistic and non-linguistic, that the infant encounters. In conclusion, the infant's so-called natural behaviours and primary biological cognitive skills are social through and through, and in this respect are more akin to what has been described as biologically secondary cognitive abilities.

Example of early social-communicative interactions:
the Peek-a-boo game, and the concepts of 'pain' and 'self'
Let me now illustrate another case of the infant's natural behaviour as a basis for symbiosis and social play. The example is the game of Peek-a-boo (Bruner, 1976). Bruner studied infants between the ages of ten and seventeen months of age and described the developmental changes as an example of 'gut' play turned into play with conventions (Bruner, 1976, p. 284).

In the beginning, this game utilises strong pre-adapted responses in young infants. The mothers studied by Bruner reported that 'looming', in which the mother approaches or looms towards the infant's face from approximately one meter and says 'Boo!', precedes the Peek-a-boo game. If the looming is directly towards the infant's face, there is a reflexive avoidance reaction, which seems to be innate. Therefore, one of the most important aspects of Peek-a-boo, that is, disappearance or avoidance, builds on the infant's reflexive behaviours. Furthermore, appearance and disappearance, the main aspects of the game, are aspects of object manipulation, and are also innately based (Piaget, 1937/1954). So in the beginning, and also as the game becomes more structured and two-sided, it is governed not only by conventional rules or norms but also by strong pre-adapted responses in the infant. These are used by the mother in the structuring of her interactions with the infant.

All Peek-a-boo games have the same basic structure of initial contact, disappearance, reappearance, and re-established contact. Initially the game involves a limited set of hiding tools, time variations, vocalisations, and so on. But as the infant matures and becomes more skilful in the game, modifications in hiding tools occur: for example, a rag, a hand, even a chair can function as the hiding tool, depending on the context. Having reached this stage in playing the game, the infant seems to master not only the rules of turn-taking, that is, appearance and disappearance, but also a wide range of variations inside a set of relatively fixed rules – 'patterned variations within constraining rules' (Bruner, 1976, p. 283). Before the age of ten to thirteen months, the mother controls the unmasking, timing, and so on, but after this age the infant begins to take control. The infant now becomes an actor in its own right and the mother a recipient, as the symbiosis begins to break up. Bruner also points out that vocalisations play a role in Peek-a-boo. In the beginning, they help the infant localise the mother's face, but they soon become parts of the game, occurring concurrently with specific behaviours and responses. This and other vocalisations by the mother help the infant make the transition from initially non-linguistic games to language games (Newson, 1978).

To sum up: the infant, by combining different skills in interaction with the caregiver, has developed the ability to take turns, co-ordinate its own actions with another, follow intersubjective and conventional rules, and master variations inside a set of relatively determined rules. At around twelve to fifteen months, the infant has acquired the skills required to participate in language games, which simply constitute other systems of conventional rules that vary to fit the context and can change if such a change is socially accepted. The infant has therefore acquired the ability or skill to communicate and to make productive use of conventional rules.

Another example of symbiotic learning can be seen if we consider how the infant learns the word 'pain', or, as in the case of the 'Baby X' experiments, words like 'fear' or 'anger'. The infant typically exhibits both bodily signs of harm (e.g., bleeding) and typical expressions of pain or anger such as crying. The mother or caregiver attends to the infant by stopping the bleeding and feeling the sore leg, but also treats and talks to the infant as if it felt pain, anger, or fear. In this way, language is attached to the natural sign, such as crying. The infant comes to imitate the use of the word and use it as part of a natural expression (i.e., as in deferred imitation or symbolic play when one thing is used to stand for something else). Eventually – and this is the crucial step – the infant uses it instead of the natural expression. Pain does not refer to pain behaviour, nor, to make a subtle Wittgensteinian point, is it used to describe a bad feeling; rather it expresses the state of the infant. It gets attached, just as the crying does, to the inner sensations, as one of their proper modes of expression. The symbiotic relationship has thus helped the infant to acquire a new skill – language – and to relate it to something naturally present. As a result, the infant can eventually express its own subjective feelings in speech.

Although the symbiotic interaction seems to be breaking up around the time the infant begins to speak, traces of it are important in the acquisition of language even at later stages. Many of the infant's first utterances are difficult if not impossible to understand, and later idiosyncratic use of words and grammatical constructions, even when correctly pronounced, leads to difficulties. Ryan (1974) and others report that mothers often respond to infants' utterances by expanding on them, adding to them and changing them. Mothers make interpretations of what the infant is saying on the basis of such things as the infant's intonation pattern, accompanying actions (e.g., pointing), and the circumstances (e.g., the absence of an object), and thereby delimit the meaning more exactly. This is illustrated by instances of baby talk.

Another illustration of how mental activity incorporates both body and culture can be given by considering self-knowledge and language. In his paper 'Five kinds of self-knowledge' (1988), Neisser argues that there are five different selves: the ecological or physical self, the interpersonal or social self, the extended or memory-related self, the private or subjective self, and the conceptual self. These selves are seldom experienced as distinct, but 'differ in their developmental histories, in the accuracy with which we can know them, in the pathologies to which they are subject, and generally in what they contribute to human experience.' (Neisser, 1988, p. 35). Thus, to think about the self as unified and as consisting of just subjective awareness of mental processes, in the way the Cartesian conception of mind suggests, is misleading. These five selves are grounded in different mechanisms, according to Neisser. The first two (at least initially) are grounded in the individual person's direct perception of the physical and social environment, i.e., are like the phonetic, syntactic, and innate social skills. But the other three also involve different aspects of cultural interaction. Consider the private self, which is made up of conscious experiences that are not available to anyone else, which is important to most human beings, and which, according to the Western tradition, is the centre of our psychological activity and being. Young children have conscious experiences; but it is only around the age of three that they notice that certain experiences seem to belong exclusively to them. This apparently indicates that the difference between public and private action and discourse is the result of a certain human practice, namely learning to keep what one thinks, feels, and so on to oneself. The adult speaks to the infant and treats it as if it already has a self in this sense. Certain behaviours are reacted to and described as if they originated from a private self.

The self as an organising principle originates from these public descriptions and reactions, and the adult helps the infant to connect language and concepts with its natural behaviours. The infant becomes able to co-ordinate its actions and experiences with those of others, and thereby acquires the further forms of self: the memory self, the private self, and the conceptual self, all depending on and varying with different socio-cultural contexts. For example, as Neisser points out, the conception of a private self seems to be typical of Western psychological functioning, but it is not found in all cultures. In addition, what is included in the conceptual self is culturally dependent; for instance, my conception of myself as Swedish, woman, opera lover, professor, and amateur chef is cultural.

The infant's acquisition of language and a cognitive system is a result of both an internal and individual framework of skills and a framework of social interactions with immanent rules of language and cognitive activities. It is a result of a social construction utilising different skills, some of which have aspects that are isomorphic with language and conceptual activities, but which could not, by themselves, be sufficient to permit the mastery of language or cognition.

Later language learning

My account of language acquisition above has been limited to the very early learning of the infant, since this is the model used by natural learning theories, but of course much language acquisition takes place after this period. This later learning is both similar to and in some respects different from earlier learning. For example, imitation skills help the infant learn words and new syntactical constructions. Through practice, speech production improves and becomes more adult around the infant's tenth birthday (Lieberman, 1984). The child's extensive social networks of peers and adults increase the mastery of the pragmatic-communicative aspects of language. In addition, language itself adds a new and powerful skill to the infant's existing set. Language can be applied to and combined with other skills as well as with itself. For instance, the child seems to move beyond non-verbal ways of social interaction to the use of folk psychology narratives to understand others (Hutto, 2008). Language also sharpens the child's capabilities in manipulating objects and enables the quick representation of different structures. With language, the child is able to plan ahead and test actions before performing them. Language also makes the infant both radically independent of adults and also able to learn from them by listening to explicit explanations. Thus, the learning situation changes and the child comes to play a larger role. Although symbiosis diminishes, it is still part of later learning, as for example in the case of apprenticeship learning (see Rogoff, 1990). Cases of symbiotic learning are found in the university classroom as well. One frequently observes the way undergraduates ask questions with words they do not fully understand. Very often, the teacher reformulates the question in an appropriate way and answers it on the basis of the reformulation. Although the subject matter is different, the situation is not really so very far from that of the mother interacting with the infant. A similar situation is also found in scientific contexts (see Jarvie, 2005; Kuhn, 1962).

Although later learning and cognitive development build on early learning and are in some respects different, they still involve socio-cultural interactions, norms, and rules. With increasing social networks, and especially in institutionalised situations for learning like schools, these rules and norms are explicitly stated, as in the case of criteria for grades, national tests, and goals of education, for example. Nevertheless, this later learning is similar to early learning in that it is socio-cultural, but this does not mean that all learning should be like early language learning. Instead this learning, like all learning, is best understood in the way that the mainstream approach describes the acquisition of secondary cognitive skills. It is symbolic, shares in cultural traditions, depends on both biology and location in time and space, and requires rules and interactions as well as linguistic or other cognitive artefacts. When the mind is seen as a socio-cultural construction put together by the individual child, adults, and the different artefacts and institutions in society, all learning is better understood as 'domestication' rather than 'infantilisation'.

This approach takes both later learning and the acquisition of early cognitive skills during infancy to be the result of a joint construction utilising neuro-physiological structures, individual skills for speech perception, and the production of other cognitive skills and social interactions with other human beings. Instead of seeing the infant, and indeed all learners, as Piaget and Gopnik and Meltzoff do, as Robinson Crusoe-like figures constructing meaningful images or norms for knowledge internally, it is best to understand these as a result of social discourses.

CONCLUSION: LEARNING AS SOCIO-CULTURAL DISCOURSE

The analysis of language acquisition above rejects the account of intentionality and normativity in terms of both individual conscious and unconscious mental processes, and natural biological processes. The meaning of words and the normativity of different linguistic activities are shaped in the social-symbiotic discourses between the adult and the infant, using language in concrete situations. In the beginning of the process, the adult supplies both the norms and the meaning, as in the case of Peek-a-boo. As the interaction proceeds, the child comes to master more and more aspects of the interaction and the cognitive tools himself or herself. But these are constantly re-negotiated in discourses as the context and conditions change.[11] The normativity and intentionality of cognitive activity and change are a result not of individual mental constructions guided by biological developmental laws, but of different discursive activities. Instead of being individual, the framework for learning and productivity is accounted for in terms of individual skills and bodily enabling conditions, as well as social interaction utilising the linguistic and cognitive system and artefacts.

Although language acquisition is a special case of early learning, this general discursive approach to learning – to the problems of productivity and the framework – can be generalised to other learning situations, as I have discussed above. It is an alternative to the Cartesian conception of mind that has guided mainstream psychology, one which focuses on individual, inner mental processes or mechanisms that, as I have shown, are unable to explain the central aspects of cognitive activity. The alternative approach implicit in the account of language acquisition suggested here, and in other studies in what has become known as discursive psychology, avoids the problems of the Cartesian approach discussed in the previous chapters.[12] It suggests that the way to approach different cognitive activities is to investigate the enabling conditions, such as neuro-physiological structures and different skills, as well as the discursive practices which 'shape' these skills and structures in accordance with socially negotiated norms.

---

[11] See for example developments in positioning theory (Harré and Moghaddam, 2003).
[12] See for example Harré (2002); Harré and Gillett (1994); Harré and Stearns (1995).

More fundamentally, this 'ideal of psychological order' takes the mind and mental activity to be both internal and external, both individually and collectively constructed, thus rejecting the Cartesian conception of mind as something individual and private. Explanations of mental activity are not reducible to physics or physiology or something else which lacks normativity and intentionality, yet explanations have to be sought in something which includes these (see Harré, 2001, for example). If the mind is understood as a set of skills and techniques, both individual and social, that renders the world meaningful to the learner and to other people at the same time, then the Cartesian conception of mind as an entity sealed into its own self-contained and subjective sphere must be thoroughly revised. We should instead see the mind and mental activity as the meeting point of a wide range of structuring influences which are jointly constructed. The study of mental activity such as learning has to take a much broader approach than the focus on the individual learner and his or her natural abilities.

Mental activity such as learning – in infancy, in schools, and at the university – is always and fundamentally embedded in specific historical, political, cultural, social, and interpersonal contexts. Mental activity such as acquiring one's first language is neither identified nor explained by looking at a shadowy and inaccessible world of mental processes. I have argued in earlier chapters that it cannot be accounted for in terms of biological laws. As I showed in the chapter on Piaget, what fixes the meaning of words and symbols cannot be hidden in the subjective and private processes of the individual. Neither can the criteria or norms of what count as knowledge. Piaget's attempt to locate the norms of cognitive growth in biological laws also fails. Norms and rules of meaning shape natural abilities in joint socio-cultural constructions in specific historical and cultural circumstances, and are not a result of universal laws of biological change.

According to this approach, early and late learning are both natural and socio-cultural and are not something that can be left to the individual child, or for that matter the scientist, to accomplish on his or her own, utilising biological structures and innately grounded skills. We need to study carefully both the enabling conditions, of which many have an innate base, and the relevant social discourses. In education, this means we must study cognition in the more limited sense of individual enabling conditions, how these change over time, and how they are relevant in different learning situations. But we also need to study the social discourses related to specific 'subject matters' that shape these enabling conditions and skills. All ordered mental change or learning, including early learning, is more like the acquisition of the so-called biologically secondary cognitive skills. Learning is always the acquisition of culturally varied concepts, language, ideas, and belief systems, and it is always taking place in a varied socio-cultural context. Furthermore, is not necessarily intrinsically motivating in the sense suggested by natural learning theories. If we see learning as a dynamic activity, which children and adults engage in together in the context of various external but socially grounded belief systems, then the focus of education becomes fundamentally different.

7   Towards discursive education

My focus has been on methodology, discussing the fundamental assumptions about mind, knowledge, and cognitive change that inform contemporary accounts of learning, and not on the actual use of computers in schools. In my case study of computers as educational technology, I have argued that mistaken ideas of mainstream psychology underlie and inform the pedagogical reasons for the educational use of computers to enhance and even to change radically the conditions for cognitive development and learning in schools. Although such mistaken views of learning are only one of the many reasons behind the use of computers in education, it is important to discuss them, since they help structure the situations in which computers are introduced, as well as learning more generally.

As an alternative, I argue that learning and cognitive development are a social symbolic activity through and through, and also a very complex activity involving many different kinds of conditions, many different levels, and many, often conflicting goals.

Let me begin with a summary of some problematic aspects of mainstream psychology's approach to learning and knowledge. I shall then sketch what a discursive approach to learning and education would involve in a more general sense. By doing this, I hope to provide the first steps towards a discursive approach to education. A more substantive account would involve moving beyond my methodological focus, and must await a subsequent book.

THE FAILURE OF NATURAL LEARNING THEORIES
It is a mistake to claim that all learning is like natural learning, namely the acquisition of what are usually thought of as primary, mostly

innate, cognitive skills. The main reason for this is that these theories fail to account for the normativity and intentionality of the framework needed for learning as well as going beyond the information given, that is, productivity. Even what has been put forth as the most typical case of natural learning – the acquisition of a first language in infancy – is more like the acquisition of secondary or culturally constituted cognitive skills. Like all culturally constituted skills, first language acquisition requires that the body already possesses enabling conditions, which are shaped by socio-cultural symbolic interactions taking place against the backdrop of different social institutions, as I have pointed out in previous chapters.

However, first language learning is different from many other skills that are typically thought of as secondary because it takes place outside formal schooling and also seems to require little explicit teaching or encouragement from others. The difference between this skill and later skills – for example, subjects learned in school like history and physics – has less to do with the difference between innate or natural skills on the one hand and cultural skills on the other, and more to do with the specific social context in which the skills are learned. Another difference involves the extent to which the rules and norms of the activity are explicitly stated. To be sure, in both cases biologically grounded skills are utilised in a social context to yield socio-cultural skills. It is the failure of natural learning theories to give the specifically socio-cultural and symbolic nature of all learning its due that has led to the infantilising of learning and education.

The underlying assumptions about mental activity in general, and about cognitive development, belief change, learning, and knowledge in particular, that inform natural learning theories are, as I have claimed above, based on the mainstream individualistic, mostly biologistic and universalistic 'ideal of psychological order'. The problems of productivity as well as those of the framework are answered in terms of individual, hidden, and biologically grounded universal psychological mechanisms. Theories like Piaget's, Gopnik and Meltzoff's, and Chomsky's of innate linguistic competence, as well as those of contemporary evolutionary psychology, all approach learning and cognitive development as a natural, biological process explicable by reference to individual endowments. Psychological activity is assumed to be private, hidden, and grounded in universal biological characteristics shared by all human beings across time, space, and circumstances. Prime examples of this include Piaget's theory, Chomsky's universal grammar, and the modular theory of the mind typical of evolutionary psychology. This is because they all claim that learning is fundamentally a biological process which should in the final analysis be understood in terms of biological adaptations, and in the case of Piaget in terms of universal biological evolutionary or developmental laws. For him, the view that development is the same across cognitive domains, in species, in the individual, and in society (see Piaget, 1950/1965/ 1995), is fundamental. In this general sense, ontogenesis might be said to repeat phylogenesis. Morss (1990), in his historical study of the biological assumptions of developmental psychology, claims that such biological assumptions are shared by almost all traditional developmental theories, including those of Stanley Hall, James Baldwin, and Sigmund Freud. My criticism of Piaget in previous chapters is thus relevant to most of developmental psychology, including contemporary evolutionary psychology.

This approach is also a fundamentally 'Robinson Crusoe' view of learning (see Gellner, 1985 , p. 107; see also Chapter 1), and is in line with the Western tradition of philosophy, in which knowledge growth is assumed to be the result of individuals confronting the world one by one within their own private minds. A parallel instance to this in the case of educational technology would be the lone child in front of a Skinner box, television set, or computer. As we have seen with Piaget, such an approach fails to account for some central aspects of mental activity, namely intentionality and normativity. When Gopnik and Meltzoff compared scientists and children, they went wrong in a similar way by missing the public and normative 'nature' of scientific and other beliefs, focusing instead on individual psychological activities.

Learning from error: Plato, Piaget, and Popper

An additional problem, which Piaget recognises but in the end fails to overcome, is the justificationist assumptions of this approach, because knowledge for him is seen as something static, resting on indubitable givens. Secure foundations, in the forms of either sense impressions, innate ideas, categories of thought, or evolutionary laws, are assumed to constitute the foundation of knowledge. Learning in this approach is really re-production and involves minimising rationality in the sense of minimising the role of the learner or scientist rather than expanding it.

Piaget claims that disequilibrium, the cognitive failure to cope with experience, induces change in one's conceptual structure and drives cognitive development and learning. Gopnik and Meltzoff also see scientists' and children's testing and rejecting of hypotheses as leading to change in beliefs. Socrates, according to Plato in his dialogues, is one of the first examples of someone trying to teach something through the elimination of mistakes or errors. Note that Socrates' midwife method of learning from difficulties and errors presupposes an active learner as well as an active teacher. One example is the case of the slave boy in the dialogue *Meno*, in which Socrates asks questions and corrects the boy's own suggestions. Many other philosophers, including Bacon and Descartes, also see the elimination of error as the way to knowledge. In Chapter 5 I briefly discussed Popper's claim that change is a result of falsification of scientific theories. According to Kuhn, in contrast, the rejection of paradigms with too many problems leads to change.

As we saw in the discursive account of language acquisition in Chapter 6, the learning of a first language is very much a process corresponding to a method of eliminating what does not fit in a particular language context. For example, the infant is initially more able than older children and adults both to discriminate and to produce speech sounds of more or less all known languages. This ability is lost around the first birthday, when the infant becomes better at producing

the phonemes of his or her own language. Learning is not only elimination but also the addition of something, which Piaget would agree
with. But what is eliminated and added is not something governed by
biology or individual mental processes, but a result of the child's active
participation in social activities like games and conversations with
implicit as well as explicit rules and norms. This is very clear in the
case of the semantic-communicative aspects of language acquisition,
where the child's natural abilities to produce and react to speech
sounds are shaped by and then utilised in social interaction. The child's
natural ability to produce most speech sounds occurring in all human
language is reduced and adjusted to the surrounding speech community. It is the adult or older child who in this way domesticates the
child's underdetermined and open-ended behaviour so that it conforms
to the language spoken around the child. Therefore Skinner was correct to stress the social context and its response to the learner's behaviour in the form of reinforcements or punishments. However, he was
mistaken to see it in simplistic terms as the conditioning of a passive
learner. In conclusion, learning from error – for example in the process
of learning a language – consists of first putting forth a speech sound,
and then 'selecting', thus learning, the appropriate one on the basis of
social interaction.

Although Plato in *The Republic* (1974) was mistaken about
many things, his division of learning into two distinct stages – the
first involving the early acquisition by imitation of basic cultural
skills, and the second learning skills that involve thinking rationally
and evaluating what is learned – is useful. It points to a distinction
between 'pure domestication' in acquiring a linguistic and cognitive
first framework, and the second-order skills necessary to be able to go
beyond this initial framework. Both these types of skills are social.
Both extend a biological being's rationality rather than reducing it, but
the second-order activity also involves the active criticism of one's
own or others' knowledge claims. It involves something that is not
intrinsically motivating, namely coping with mistakes and the

possibility of change in the face of uncertainty. To find ways to encourage this second-order skill and to motivate the learner to extend his or her reasoning in this way is perhaps the most central challenge for schools, rather than attempting to turn them back into infants. This later bias is because schoolchildren (and adults), like infants, seem to seek and enjoy regularities, such as playing Peek-a-boo, and are resistant to uncertainty and change. They try to reduce or select what is relevant in their 'natural' productivity with the help of others, and thereby to conform to what is socially accepted. The challenge for schools is to encourage the critical second-order skills of the pupils. Let me clarify this by pointing to some important, but in certain respects flawed, insights of Piaget's, and comparing them to Popper's views on knowledge and the growth of knowledge.

Learning from error: Popper's evolutionary epistemology
succeeds where Piaget's genetic epistemology fails
Popper and Piaget were contemporaries and both developed evolutionary epistemologies, but in spite of some similarities, these have very different views about the growth of knowledge. One difference has already been alluded to, namely the role of social interaction in scientific thinking (Chapter 5), but there are even more important differences. Before presenting these, let me point to similarities in their approaches to the growth of knowledge.

Both Popper and Piaget see knowledge and its growth as adaptation to the environment, enabling humans to go beyond animals through their cognitive abilities, and both see the organism and individual learner as being actively involved in seeking out and constructing his or her own beliefs or hypotheses about the world. Furthermore, both also take perception and cognition to be in constant flux. A later experience is never the repetition of an earlier one, even if the stimuli are the same (see Popper, 1957; Piaget, 1980). Both assume that the individual makes unwarranted generalisations, conjectures, and other mistakes – fallibility of knowledge claims in Popper's case and mistaken causal generalisations in Piaget's. Learning occurs by error reduction in Popper's view and by restoring imbalances in Piaget's, which is to say that for both learning is a process of selection. They also view knowledge as something that is embedded in a process, something constantly changing, and both deny what Popper refers to as the 'truth is manifest' assumption in traditional rationalism and empiricism.

In spite of these similarities, they end with different views of learning and the growth of knowledge. Some of the differences can be explained by their different views of evolution, given Piaget's pre-Darwinian, metaphysical assumption of evolutionary progress and Popper's neo-Darwinism. As I have shown, the learner both for Piaget and in natural learning theories is seen to be pre-programmed by evolutionary and innate laws to respond to the environment in specific ways, leading to knowledge claims that are more and more certain. This reduces the deliberative and active aspect of human reason to biological responses, akin to an animal's immediate and adaptive response to the environment. Popper's view is quite different and stresses deliberation and uncertainty.

Popper's most fundamental claim is that knowledge grows not through the building up of certain information, but through constant problem solving by tentative generalisations, knowledge claims, or conjectures and the continual correction and rejection of these in the face of difficulties. The learner is actively engaged in problem solving and constructing tentative solutions, which are then revised or rejected if the evidence runs contrary to them. In this sense, knowledge is a series of moments in a process. Piaget, in contrast, explicitly refers to knowledge as stages in a process and is critical of traditional epistemologies because they present the growth of knowledge as a representation of certain foundations. Yet he himself ended, as we have seen, in a similar position, with evolutionary laws as the secure foundations of knowledge which produce certainty, objectivity, and truth over time. Popper rejects both the justificationism of Piaget and that of traditional epistemologies. Truth is something we strive for, but not something we could ever know even if we had achieved it. Truth or certainty of beliefs is neither the starting point nor the manifest end result of the process of attempting to acquire knowledge. Learning has to take place without this, and proceeds by active construction and constant criticism of what one has come up with. This criticism is not something the individual engages in by himself or herself, but is the social activity of critical discussion. It has to be social, because what it criticises is not the individual's private beliefs, but the (objective) content of these beliefs, beliefs which are social through and through (see Chapter 5 above). Therefore learning and the growth of knowledge, although grounded in human biology, go beyond it. Humans are born non-rational, but become rational by constant construction and criticism, by extending and refining their purely animal skills in a social and cultural context. This is not an easy process, according to Popper (see for example Bailey, 2000; see also Berkson and Wetterstein, 1984), since humans, especially infants and children, want and actively seek regularities. Early learning, especially language learning, helps the child order his or her unordered and instinct-based animal skills, and this makes learning motivating, as I have shown. But the learning of a second-order skill like critical discussion is different. Children very often resist learning and applying it, because it involves constructing, testing, changing, and rejecting beliefs in the face of uncertainty, since there are no criteria of truth or any certain or necessary foundations. This, as I said above, poses a challenge for schools, and is not solved by treating children as if they were infants.

The fact that there are more dogmatic types of learning as well as critical or scientific types suggests a way to approach learning in schools. Children have to learn many things dogmatically – as in the case of being domesticated into their first language – in order for them to have an initial shared framework, but learning does not end there. The most crucial and difficult skill in later cognitive development is the acquisition and utilisation of critical discussion. This is not inherently motivating and is very much dependent on the child's active interest and willingness to solve problems. Thus education has to be child centred, but not in the way natural learning theories see it.

Schools have to afford a context that induces both types of learning. Critical learning is especially difficult because it also requires that the child be encouraged to question not only his or her own beliefs and ideas, but those of other pupils, as well as those of the teacher. If this reasoning is correct, it points to a more useful distinction than the one between learning natural, primary, cognitive skills and later cultural-symbolic skills (see the discussion in Chapter 1), namely the distinction between dogmatic and critical learning skills. Both are symbolic and socio-cultural, but they are subject to different norms as well as skills and motivations on the part of the pupil.

In sum: Piaget is correct in many of his basic ideas and criticisms of traditional epistemologies, but his theory fails as a whole because of a mistaken conception of mind, knowledge, and evolution. Individualism, historicism, and justificationism are the source of his basic mistakes, because they minimise the role of the learner and of his or her intelligence. Learning is reduced to something outside the control of individuals (as in the case of Piaget's epistemic subject) and beyond human deliberation and choice, thereby making us less than human. The discursive approach, on the other hand, claims that both first-order and second-order learning extend natural beings beyond their biological limitations so that they become cultural and social beings, beings who learn from, criticise, and change their shared framework and also create lasting expressions of it in the form of books, films, computer programs, and the like.

DISCURSIVE LEARNING

There are three sets of conditions or frameworks for learning, which are at one and the same time enabling and limiting conditions, that educators have to consider. First, there are those set by the human body and especially the brain. Second, there are those set by varying socio-cultural interactions and norms, expressed in activities like games and conversations. Third, there is the content of the cognitive systems themselves, expressed in books, films, computers – what Karl Popper calls the 'third world' (Popper, 1972). The human brain with its special structure and way of functioning can perform certain sorts of information processing which are categorically different from what can be done by a computer (for example see Harré, 2001). But the social interactions and content of the cognitive culture set the outer limits and possibilities that are relevant for mental activity at any given time and place. Instead of constituting a branch of biology, as Piaget thought, psychology and educational theory as well are hybrid sciences involving physiology, primarily neuro-physiology, and socio-historical disciplines (Gardner, 2004; for an example of such studies see Harré and Stearns, 1995).

As I have shown in the previous chapters, language acquisition is not a natural process, even though it involves many innately based biological abilities or skills such as speech, perception, and what appears to be the natural social disposition of infants. Such natural abilities or skills are shaped and ordered by the semantic-symbolic and communicative interactions supported by the linguistic context of the community in which adults involve the child. Children learn to talk in a social context involving specific social interactions, like the Peek-a-boo game. Such games take place in specific linguistic settings at specific times, for example in contemporary Swedish or Japanese households. In this way, the child's natural or feral productivity, which itself is productive in the sense of being underdetermined, is shaped in accordance with prevailing but culturally and historically varying rules and norms. The framework that enables learning and cognitive development requires individual and natural skills, like the ability to produce speech sounds, which are shaped by specific social linguistic interaction or discourse (e.g., in a Swedish family). The framework that provides the starting point as well as the norms is not only individual; it is public and shared, and, most importantly, is transmitted in linguistic interactions and exchanges. The child's behaviour and socio-culturally shaped interactions with others, who interpret and act towards the child in specific ways guided by social roles and norms, provide the framework for learning. Such norms and rules are in most cases not explicitly stated, nor are they hidden in individual minds, but are immanent in the social interactions and the socio-cultural institutions that shape them (see Harré, 2000, 2002). In later learning, some of these rules and norms are explicitly stated, as in curricula, grading criteria, etc., but this does not change the fundamental conditions for learning. It is a process of discursive domestication, rather than infantilisation.

To claim that cognitive activity like learning is discursive is to claim that the framework for all mental activity consists of individual participation in and contributions to the context of public linguistic and cognitive activities.

Furthermore, to engage in discursive activity is to engage in joint intentional and normative cognitive activity using symbols. Discursive activities include such things as conversations, argumentation, discussion, games like Peek-a-boo, and other social activities involving the public display and use of norms. Discursive activities like discussion and argumentation require a language and a related social context, often involve the questioning and changing of beliefs and knowledge claims, and are therefore productive in the sense that scientific activity is productive. Such activity is an important part of second-order cognitive activity, that is, cognitive activity which addresses cognitive ideas and claims. In discursive acts like conversations and teaching, but also sports, arts activities, etc., norms and rules emerge in historical and cultural circumstances and make something not only meaningful, but also right or wrong to do, learn, think, or feel. Think for example about how the rules for tennis have changed over time, or how art was different in Ancient Egypt and in the late nineteenth century in Paris.

Discursive activities not only transmit and structure what people do and learn when they change their behaviour and beliefs. Discourse also includes publicly recorded and publicly displayed cognitive activities in linguistic form, such as books or a dissertation, thesis, tract, monograph or treatise.[1] To become a skilled participant

---

[1] Here again I am thinking of what Popper (1972) refers to as the 'third world'.

in such an activity involves domesticating or adjusting one's natural and underdetermined skills to those of the cognitive community, but also requires one to question, criticise, and change cognitive claims and systems. Thus it involves the ability to engage in what I have called second-order cognitive activity. By engaging in these activities – which first are directed and shaped by others but in which with increasing skill one can be an active participant – one becomes rational. Think of a child learning to read and write, moving from confused and unsystematic behaviour to mastery, understanding, and creativity. While Piaget is correct to claim that the productivity of cognitive activity is unordered in the beginning but gets ordered in the course of development and learning, he is mistaken in attributing this to biological invariants or laws.

A well-formed and healthy human body and brain are important preconditions for cognition, providing the basis for underdetermined productivity but also constituting a limitation to the kind of socio-cultural skills that can be developed. Of course, what counts as 'healthy' is related to the norms of acceptable performances in a given culture. Humans, however, can only develop certain cognitive and other skills and cannot perform the same tasks as, for example, a hunting dog, or for that matter a computer, or an artificial intelligence system. Many of these bodily conditions are universal in that they are more or less the same, in normal cases, for all humans. These are enabling conditions, just as the human body and the tennis racket are enabling conditions for tennis, but the game of tennis is not reduced to physiological and physical mechanisms of the body and the tennis racket; it is instead a result of conforming to the norms involved in the game and the uses the players make of their bodies and rackets. One cannot serve except in a game of tennis with its specific rules. These rules or norms change over time and also with place. While it is important to be aware of bodily enabling conditions, reductive explanations that focus on these alone are unsatisfactory, as I have shown in the discussion of Piaget's account of learning, because they fail to account for the intentionality and normativity of cognitive activities.

A related mistake is to account for mental activity by reference to inner, hidden, and private activity in the form of mental representations, like understanding and memory. Wittgenstein is correct when he argues that in order to account for mental activities like remembering, thinking, language learning, or even reading, we need not refer to inner, hidden mental processes. As we have seen above (especially in Chapters 4 and 5), such processes only reproduce on an inner, hidden, unobservable level the very characteristics that are to be explained. Wittgenstein does not deny that there are subjective experiences, only that they lack explanatory value, as we saw when I discussed Piaget's account of the emergence of intentionality. Furthermore, Wittgenstein argues that subjective experiences of mental representations are not a primary characteristic of mental activity, but rather are the result of public discourse. Instead of focusing on only one (derived) aspect of the framework, namely inner, hidden mental processes, we should be looking at the social conditions and interactions that are transmitted and actually form the individual activity and subjective experience. This is not to deny subjectivity, but to claim that instead of its being primary and the foundation on which cognition and cognitive change rest, it is the result of social and public activity.

Vygotsky's account of cognitive change, which describes it as the internalisation of public discursive acts, provides a better view of what happens when someone learns something (Vygotsky, 1934/1994). His idea of the appropriation of the collective and public into the individual and private, as in the example of social speech turning into egocentric speech and eventually into private thinking, is a more fruitful way to account for learning. The account provided in the previous chapter on language acquisition is an application of his and Wittgenstein's approach. Initially, public language is used in interactions when the adult functions as an interpreter of the child's behaviours and reactions. Later, the child uses the learned speech to control others. Later still, so-called egocentric speech, talking aloud to oneself, is used to control the child's own actions. Finally, speech is internalised and becomes thought. The child also comes to question and change the knowledge claims which were dogmatically accepted as part of early learning. In this way, concepts like the 'self' are culturally and socially transmitted, forming the child's own reactions and later the ordering of his or her subjective experiences. When concepts are internalised, although socially transmitted and formed, they become idiosyncratic and subjective. Thus the subjective self, or our awareness of ourselves as having specific characteristics distinct from others, although socially formed and transmitted, is not a replica of the external self and in a sense goes beyond the information which has been socially provided about who and what one is. In education, this process of appropriation is constantly taking place in the zone of proximal development, and the teacher, social interactions, and the norms they transmit are crucial for this reason.

When concepts or beliefs are internalised, they change, and the child is able to develop and go beyond the teacher in individualising the socially acquired. If the pupil then chooses, he or she can bring the individually altered concepts or beliefs into the public domain, and, if accepted in some discursive context, the new concepts, beliefs, etc. become part of the public and collective sphere. Examples of this are the emergence of new words or games in the school playground. Both the first- and second-order cognitive changes relevant to learning and schooling take place in this collective and public sphere of discursive activity. This educational discursive context, in which the child actively engages together with others, 'decides' what can be meaningfully and properly said and done. This activity is best described as discursive, since it involves symbolic activity, and is constitutive of language that is used in particular contexts – what Wittgenstein called language games.

One useful model of how to approach and analyse discourses in learning situations like the ones occurring in schools is found in positioning theory, a development of Goffman's dramaturgical model of face-to-face social interactions.[2] This theory develops Vygotsky's

---

[2] See for example Goffman (1974); Harré and Moghaddam (2003); Harré and van Langehove (1999).

insight that psychological processes are appropriated from public interactions, and the later Wittgenstein's views of mental processes, out-
lined above. Positioning theory acknowledges the context dependence
and constant change of psychological activity and also stresses the
wider social context as well as the contents of relevant symbol systems, like texts, laws, etc. The focus is on the study of the nature,
formation, influence, and change of local systems of rights and duties
of the participants in specific social interactions. In an educational
context, the analysis also needs to focus not only on how pupils are
positioned with respect to their rights and duties as learners, but also
on how these are connected to ideas about the learner's capacities. For
example, it would make a difference to the learning situation of a pupil
whether he or she is seen as rational and capable of decisions or, as
natural learning theories assume, as governed by universal and
unchanging biological laws. Thus, psychological theories matter and
need to be discussed and analysed as part of any effort to understand
and improve the educational situation. This is one motivation for my
highly critical discussion of natural learning theories. But a discursive
approach to education has to encompass more: the study of rights and
duties, of laws and other relevant texts, as well as face-to face interactions. What I have attempted is to discuss only one aspect, namely
the assumptions that are made about the psychological characteristics
of pupils.

The discursive approach involves seeing the learner not as a
solitary individual, but instead as one contributor among others who
is becoming more and more skilled in different discourses and at tasks
that are cognitive. That learning is an instance of domestication may at
first sight appear to turn the matter of some of unique human characteristics – cognition, language, and science – into something biological
or animal-like, thereby reducing educational activities which promote
individual growth and self-realisation, rationality, decision-making,
and responsibility, to something akin to the training of animals. But
it is precisely the natural learning approach, rather than the alternative
suggested here, that biologises and also infantilises education by seeing

children as primarily biological beings, thereby undermining our socio-cultural heritage of discourse about ideas and beliefs. It is undermined because this approach reduces cognitive activity and rationality to something biological like the innate abilities that are the products of evolution, thereby minimising the individual's own cognitive contribution and intelligence.[3] But learning and cognitive development are meant to expand the role of reason or intelligence, not reduce it. This is clearly the case with the kind of domestication involved in acquiring a language, because it turns a purely natural being with innate abilities into a language-using human being. It is also the case with the second-order cognitive skills that are essential if we are to criticise and change or go beyond knowledge already acquired, or the wider cognitive context and system into which one has been domesticated. This learning, as well as domestication, involves an active individual either selecting what to believe or learning from error.

TOWARDS DISCURSIVE EDUCATION

All learning, both late and early, is a discursive undertaking; cognitive change is always a social process in which both the form it takes and the content involved are culturally and historically varied. Learning and cognitive development involve the domestication, not infantilisation, of the learner. Natural enabling conditions are always involved, but the longer learning proceeds the less important these become. When the child has acquired his or her first language, this language – which is to some extent individually appropriated – is important in shaping all future cognitive growth. Acquiring a language is the most important precondition for taking part in symbolic activities, especially in schooling. But schooling also involves other skills, such as the ability to ascribe beliefs to others and meta-cognition, the second-order ability to reflect on and criticise one's own and others' cognitive activities both publicly and privately. This involves the awareness of

---

[3] See Fuller (2003) for a short discussion of how Bruner, among others, has contributed to reducing the role of intelligence.

one's own beliefs in relation to the norms and standards set and agreed to by teachers or others with institutional authority. In this important sense, what is private and individual is secondary. Publicly giving and accepting reasons for beliefs, explaining them, and acquiring consent for them are almost universal features of schooling (see Olson, 2003), so schooling is in a sense the discursive activity *par excellence.*

Some of the norms for teaching and learning are explicitly and publicly stated. For example, in many subjects specific goals for learn-ing are stated in schoolbooks and also tested in national exams. However, many norms or limiting conditions for the mental activity taking place in schools are less explicit, yet also function to organise the way we think about pupils and what they can learn. Although these beliefs are historically and culturally situated, they can be thought of as transcendental in the sense that they depend on organising concepts which form not only our beliefs but also a whole body of practices (see Hacking, 2002). These seem inescapable and are very often not explic-itly stated but function rather like depth knowledge, much as Chomsky's deep grammar is assumed to function in language learning and use.

As already mentioned, one such set of beliefs includes the belief discussed in this book, namely the idea of learning that is assumed by natural learning theories. We have seen in the discussion of computers as educational technology that the fundamental assumptions are sel-dom stated, yet underlie most discussions of computer use. Such assumptions influence not only teachers' interactions with pupils, but also the way schools are organised, subject matters chosen, grading goals formulated, course evaluations worked out, funding given or withheld, staffing cut or enlarged, and the like. Most important, they also influence the way that pupils see themselves as learners, that is, as natural beings following their biological developmental course. Discussing these basic assumptions is thus very important, since they not only form the pedagogy and the actual social encounters in schools, but also influence the minds of the learners; not only do these assumptions form the learning situation in the classroom or elsewhere, but they also affect the very cognitive skills, like reading, that are acquired. By seeing learning as a purely natural process, we minimise the role of cognition and reason. Instead, we should be discussing how humans are able to expand their powers of reason by combining what is a natural endowment with different cultural achievements.

Therefore, to understand learning and cognitive growth, particularly in formal schooling, we need to understand the skills and social interactive settings that prepare children for school, such as language acquisition, developing an ability to understand the thoughts and feelings of others, and getting a grasp of meta-cognition – the capacity to think about our thoughts and actions. But it is no less important to understand the school as a social institution which provides different, socially shaping conditions for learning, and to understand in which respects it is similar and dissimilar to other situations affording cognitive growth. But very little of general interest can be said about these conditions because they vary across time and place.

In proposing his stage theory of cognitive development, Piaget stresses something that is of fundamental importance in all cases of cognitive development, namely that the entities studied in the psychology of cognitive change do not retain their characteristics over time. When one learns something, one's cognitive skill is changed and becomes different from what it was before; therefore one's mental content and ability are changed, and are not the same over time. Piaget argues, as we have seen, that the traditional epistemological approaches to cognitive growth – empiricism as well as rationalism – have a static and truth-preserving view of knowledge growth. He rejects this view as too static, one that does not reflect the dynamics of cognitive growth, in particular the ability to go beyond the information given. However, he fails to account for normative productivity by proposing a biological basis for the growth of knowledge. In Piaget's view, although the individual changes over time, he or she changes according to some biologically invariant laws of growth and belief change, laws which are universal and which result in rigidly ordered stages and a fixed end state. Socially grounded and changing standards of correctness, propriety, etc. have no place in his system.

The discursive approach adds to the insight that cognition constantly changes and the fact that it also varies with the socio-cultural context. It is also an open-ended quest, one where there is no certainty. Not only does the individual learner change over time, but so do the social institutions in which he or she is embedded, like language, schools, economies, political systems, etc. Think of the Soviet Union after the revolution compared to tsarist Russia, or of the change in schools when corporal punishment was abolished. The conditions for face-to-face social interactions also change. Imagine, for example, an Afghan classroom with and without the veil. Furthermore, which subject matters are appropriate to learning change, in particular their specific content or claims? In addition, the ideals and theories of learning and cognitive development change. As an example, behaviourism was replaced by constructivism. With the exception of certain conditions, like fundamental limitations of the human brain and body, both enabling and 'shaping' conditions vary across time and place. This is the case for all forms of psychological activity, such as remembering and the display of emotions (see for example Harré and Stearns, 1995).

Add to this the multiplicity of varying norms and goals that are found in different times and places and, indeed, often at the same time and place, and we have a most complex situation. It is a situation that provides little basis for proposing universal claims about learning and teaching. The dream of finding easy and universally applicable solutions, which is so prevalent in, for example, leading US technological reforms of education is fundamentally mistaken. It is no surprise that Evans (1979) points out that in spite of thousands of years of trying to understand education, we still know very little of what goes on when a teacher teaches and a pupil learns. According to the discursive approach to cognitive growth and learning, there is simply *no* best method or technology which works in all contexts, yet this dream has long prevailed and still does so as strongly as ever, for example in the hopes that were proposed for the new computer technology.

With this complexity in mind, it becomes easier to understand why there are so many examples of educational reforms that are successful locally, but fail when 'exported' (see Olson, 2003). It is, I think, one reason why some scholars, like Hamlyn (1978), describe later learning in schools as an art rather than a science. By this he means that the relationship between the teacher and the learner depends on many different conditions that vary across cultures, times, and specific contexts. The goals of teaching, what is taught, whether it is a skill or the content of a subject matter, which technique is appropriate to its transmission, the level at which it is taught, the sort of persons being taught, or the circumstances and locale in which the teaching is taking place all vary. There is no such thing as a simple goal for teaching, a uniform context, one technique or method, or the same conditions for success. Bruner writes 'You cannot strip learning of its content, nor study it in a "neutral" context. It is always situated, always related to some ongoing enterprise. Perhaps there is no such thing as "learning in general"' (Bruner, 2004, p. 20).

An additional matter further complicates attempts to understand, namely the fact that the teacher has to do many other things besides teaching, like keeping order, getting the students' attention, etc. Instead of looking for simple solutions, including technological ones like the use of computers, it is more illuminating to confine oneself to specific discourses of teaching at particular times and places. Thus, the role of scientific theories of child development, although helpful, is only one of the factors that one has to consider.

This is not to say that student-centred education makes no sense, but that focusing only on some of the student's abilities – as natural learning theories do with their infantilisation of education – misses what is important, namely the historically and culturally situated social interactions and the norms for meaning and for what is appropriate. The child's natural and underdetermined behavioural productivity is turned into an ordered productivity because it is shaped and restricted by a framework which encompasses the child and its behaviours, as well as the social situation in which these are utilised and changed.

Given this, what can then be said, from the standpoint of the discursive approach, which will help us to understand and shape learning situations? There is very little in the form of general positive suggestions that can be made in advance of confronting particular situations. However, this is not something that needs to be viewed negatively if it helps us to sort out better how to approach something as complex and dynamic as education, clearly a 'moving target' to say the very least. It is valuable to know where not to aim as a start: understanding learning is not primarily understanding something that is hidden, individual, or biological. Instead, we must look at particular situations and contexts, particularly at the social interactive processes and varying cultural conditions. For example, the challenge facing the educational use of computers is neither a technological one nor primarily one of looking inside the pupil's head or satisfying biological conditions. What is required is that we look for relevant and effective social interactions as well as shared norms and goals of education, that is, at all aspects of the internal as well as the external framework. Of course we need to study and understand how children acquire skills, including the theory of mind and meta-cognition (see Hutto, 2008), but we need to study these in a social context and thus to come to understand the school as a social institution of a special kind.

For example (see Olson, 2003), schools are not an extension of the family or everyday social situations, but a special, social, bureaucratic institution functioning in a complex context of many other interacting social institutions. Schools reflect the needs of economic, legal, and political institutions in the larger society. These mediate between individuals and the law, the government, the economy, etc. Schools assume the task of devising, implementing, and assessing means for fulfilling the needs of those other institutions as well as promoting individual growth and development. The beliefs and ideas that pupils are responsible for in schools are different from everyday beliefs in that school-based knowledge claims usually appear in a documentary form where meanings are fixed by explicit definitions, utterances are judged by explicit standards, one has to give reasons, etc. Schooling is about domestication in specific cultural institutions using the natural as well as culturally acquired skills and beliefs of all participants. Schools are different from early symbiotic interactions because the teacher has a different role and uses different methods, such as instruction in smaller groups. Pupils are not, and cannot in the modern school be treated as, individual persons, even with the help of computers. Pupils are responded to by others as though they were more or less acting out formal, idealised roles.

Like all social contexts involving cognitive growth, schools provide and implement norms and standards for acceptable belief change and the acquisition of skills. It is not up to the pupil to determine whether he or she is able to read or spell or do multiplication (even if we appear to be moving in this direction!). The norms are social and to a large extent impersonal and institutional compared to those found in early symbiotic interactions. Yet there are also many close, even symbiotic-like relationships, with, for example, peers and sometimes with teachers as well. Schools also involve many and varied types of social actors, which are as important as, if not more important than, the teacher, such as peers (see Rich Harris, 1998).

Learning is social in its crucial aspects, as the discursive approach claims. Furthermore, learning and teaching are a complex activity changing over time and place, and there are no simple solutions to schooling. One can construct models that one knows are simplified and false, and test and improve them, but they are not generalisations applicable everywhere. They have to be applied with the help of familiarity with the special conditions in a specific time and place. This has to be kept in mind when discussing educational technologies like computers.

As we have seen in the foregoing chapter, and as became increasingly clear while working on this book (see for example Cuban, 2001), computers as educational technology have failed to live up to the early hopes of educators (see Chapter 2). They have failed just like earlier technologies, and in similar ways, by not leading to more effective teaching or learning except in a few contexts, and they are not used by the majority of teachers as tools for enhancing learning (see Chapter 2). The failure of many kinds of educational technology is not easy to explain, as Cuban (2001) has shown. Cuban presents several different possible explanations; for example, that change is a slow process, that teachers have been too little involved, and that the technologies do not meet the everyday demands of the classroom. Implicit in Cuban's discussion is the importance of the social context both in the classroom and in society at large. According to the discursive approach, this is the crucial aspect to focus on, not the individual learner. Computers, in particular the Internet, are social tools and need to be seen in a discursive context. How do they shape the child's wild productivity and how do they change the social interactions, the duties and rights, of teachers and pupils? These elements need to be analysed as part of the external social framework shaping children's cognition.

The complexity of the situation in schools should also warn us against seeing technology as an 'easy fix', something that can be generalised from a few successful cases to all or almost all instances of education (see for example Papert, 1993). Educational technology like computers should be used selectively and with care, and is able, in common with other tools like books, blackboards, pens, etc., to aid the education process. The problem is not with computers, but with how they are utilised. Natural learning theories assume that the individual child on his or her own is able to learn. And thus they are not interested in computers, their cognitive content, or how they are utilised in specific situations to learn different subject matters. This is a mistake, one which at least partly explains the failure of computers as educational tools.

One of the most challenging tasks for institutional learning, including formal learning in schools, is to motivate the learner. I think that one very important reason why natural learning theories have looked to infant learning is the fact that in this case, and uniquely, we do not seem to have to motivate the learner to learn. Infants seem to enjoy learning just as they enjoy playing. So if older children enjoy playing computer games, why not use them in schools as well? And if Piaget is correct, and all learning that occurs in natural situations is inherently motivated by attempts to restore equilibrium, why not recreate such situations with the use of computers? This seems to be the major motivation behind this approach. Achieving quick and easy satisfaction and immediate results is seen as a crucial element in learning, yet schools with standard pedagogies of learning again and again fail to motivate pupils. Why not then work with computers?

But motivating someone is not necessarily achieved by allowing him or her to have fun here and now, or by getting quick feedback to him or her, or seeing immediate positive results. Few achievements, either in sports or the arts (like opera singing, ballet dancing, or playing an instrument) or in scientific activity, would have been possible simply by imitating the infant's unique learning situation.

How then do we motivate pupils to engage in tasks that result in learning? Clearly, this has to be approached in terms of domestication, with education seen as a discursive process. What is motivating is not universal, but varies with local culture and is part of both face-to-face interactions and the wider social institutional context. We should not be looking for universal theories of hidden psychological processes allegedly inherent in all learners, but instead to the specific social context, specific subject matter, and specific learners. Furthermore, and most important, we should also look at social situations and social interactions that are conducive to learning.

While Piaget is correct that disequilibrium is important for learning, it is not an internal, natural, 'biological equilibrium' that motivates, but instead the demands of the situation in which the pupil finds himself or herself. In addition, students have to be motivated to do something which moves them forwards, rather than reverting to what is already known. Achieving this willingness to learn something new, to decide to cope with difficulties in one's beliefs, and to change them in the face of uncertainty is the real challenge for schools. And again, there are no easy answers or general solutions.

CONCLUSION

The aim of this work has not been to criticise the educational use of computers per se, but instead to make explicit and critically evaluate some of the ideas of learning assumed by what I have called the mainstream 'ideal of psychological order', in particular individualism, universalism, biologism, and justificationism. I have tried to do this by discussing theories of learning currently in vogue in the literature on the educational use of computers, ones which I have described as natural learning theories. My primary focus has been on some basic and central assumptions in Jean Piaget's approach to learning and cognitive development which inform such theories. I have argued that Piaget and natural learning theories are mistaken in their solutions to the two problems of learning: the problem of the framework and the problem of productivity. These theories minimise the role of human cognition and rationality by infantilising learning, which is viewed as the expression of innately grounded biological abilities shared by all humans. Instead, I argue that learning and cognitive development involve not only typically human biological abilities but also – and crucially – social and cultural interactions and cognitive artefacts. Both learning and teaching are involved in these processes. The conditions for teaching and learning vary locally and over time. Pedagogical generalisations are only tentative solutions to specific problem situations. The dream of a general theory of learning and simple solutions to the problem of learning in schools – which has, as I have shown, informed the pedagogical motivations of those who support the use of computers – is one reason why computers have, on the whole, so far failed to enhance learning and therefore failed as an educational technology. Infantilising and biologising the learner, and seeing learning as something that is simple and unproblematic, treat both pupils and teachers as essentially passive in the face of technology.

As an alternative to the mainstream 'ideal of psychological order' I have proposed that we adopt, at least tentatively, a discursive approach to the mind, to knowledge, and to learning. The framework for learning and for the growth of knowledge is not something that is private and hidden in individuals, but extends beyond the individual to social and discursive interactions with others and with cultural artefacts, like languages, books, and, of course, computers as well.

Appendix

Journals reviewed (all issues) 1990–9:

Classroom Computer Learning
Cognitive Development
Computers and Education
Contemporary Educational Psychology
Educational Computing and Technology
Educational Media International
Educational Philosophy and Theory
Educational Psychologist
Educational Technology
Electronic Learning
Historical Studies in Education
Instructional Science
Interchange
Journal of Computer Assisted Learning
Journal of Computer-Based Instruction
Journal of Computing in Childhood Education (not complete)
Lingua Franca
OUTPUT: Educational Computing Organization of Ontario
Performance Improvement (formerly *Performance and Instruction*)
Psychology in Schools
Technology and Learning
Tech Trends for Leaders in Education and Training
THE (Technological Horizons in Education) Journal

Database searches:

ERIC 1990–9
PSYCHINFO 1990–9

References

Antaki, C. 2004. Reading minds or dealing with interactional implications? *Theory & Psychology*, **14** (5), 667–84.

Arbib, M. A. 2005. From monkey-like action recognition to human language: an evolutionary framework for neurolinguistics. *Behavioral and Brain Sciences*, **28** (2), 105–24.

Armstrong, A. and C. Casement. 1998. *The Child and the Machine: Why Computers May Put Our Children's Education at Risk*. Beltsville, MD: Robins Lane Press.

Astington, J. W. and J. A. Baird (eds.). 2005. *Why Language Matters for Theory of Mind*. New York: Oxford University Press.

Bailey, R. 2000. *Education in the Open Society: Karl Popper and Schooling*. Aldershot: Ashgate.

Baldwin, D. 2000. Interpersonal understanding fuels knowledge acquisition. *Current Directions in Psychological Science*, **9** (2), 40–5.

Baron-Cohen, S. 1995. *Mindblindness: An Essay on Autism and Theory of Mind*. Cambridge, MA: MIT Press.

Berkson, W. and J. Wetterstein. 1984. *Learning from Error: Karl Popper's Psychology of Learning*. La Salle, IL: Open Court.

Berliner, D. and R. Calfee. 1996. *Handbook of Educational Psychology*. New York: Macmillan.

Beth, E. W., Mays, W., and J. Piaget. 1957. *Epistémologie génétique et recherche psychologique*. Paris: Presses Universitaires de France.

Bijeljac-Babic, B. J., Bertocini, J., and J. Mehler. 1993. How do 4-day-old infants categorize multisyllabic utterances? *Developmental Psychology*, **29** (4), 711–21.

Binder, C. 1993. Behavioral fluency: a new paradigm. *Educational Technology*, October, 8–14.

Blaffer Hrdy, S. 2009. *Mothers and Others: Evolutionary Origins of Mutual Understanding*. Cambridge, MA: Harvard University Press.

Bloom, P. 2004. *Descartes' Baby: How the Science of Child Development Explains What Makes Us Human*. New York: Basic Books.

Bloor, D. 1983. *Wittgenstein: A Social Theory of Knowledge*. New York: Columbia University Press.

Bowd, A., McDougall, D., and **C. Yewchuck**. 1997. *Educational Psychology for Canadian Teachers*. Toronto: Harcourt and Brace.

Bower, T. G. R. 1977. *The Perceptual World of the Child*. Cambridge, MA: Harvard University Press.

Bringuier, J-C. 1980. *Conversations with Jean Piaget*. Chicago: University of Chicago Press.

Bruner, J. 1971. *The Relevance of Education*. Harmondsworth: Penguin.

1976. Peek-a-boo and the learning of rule structures. In **J. Bruner, A. Jolly**, and **K. Sylvia** (eds.), *Play: Its Role in Development and Evolution*. Harmondsworth: Penguin.

1983. *Child's Talk: Learning to Use Language*. New York: Norton.

1990. *Acts of Meaning*. Cambridge, MA: Harvard University Press.

1996. *The Culture of Education*. Cambridge, MA: Harvard University Press.

2004. A short history of psychological theories of learning. *Daedalus*, Winter, 13–20.

Burbules, N. and **T. Callister, Jr.**, 2000. *Watch IT*. Boulder, CO: Westview Press.

Buss, D. M. 1999. *Evolutionary Psychology: The New Science of the Mind*. Boston: Allyn and Bacon.

(ed.). 2005. *Handbook of Evolutionary Psychology*. Hoboken, NJ: John Wiley & Sons.

Campbell, R. J. 1998. Hyperminds for hyper times: the demise of rational, logical thought? *Educational Technology*, January–February, 24–31.

Carruthers, P. and **P. Smith** (eds.). 1996. *Theories of Theories of Mind*. Cambridge: Cambridge University Press.

Changeux, J-P. 1985. *Neuronal Man*. New York: Pantheon.

Chapman, M. 1988. *Constructive Evolution: Origins and Development of Piaget's Thought*. New York: Cambridge University Press.

Chiou, G-F. 1992. Situated learning, metaphors and computer-based learning environments. *Educational Technology*, August, 7–11.

Chomsky, N. 1959. Review of B. F. Skinner's 'Verbal Behavior'. *Language*, **35**, 26–58.

1968. *Language and Mind*. New York: Harcourt, Brace, and World.

1975. *Reflections on Language*. New York: Random House.

1980. *Rules and Representations*. New York: Columbia University Press.

1997a. Language and cognition. In **D. M. Johnson** and **C. E. Erneling** (eds.), *The Future of the Cognitive Revolution*. New York: Oxford University Press.

1997b. Language from an internalist perspective. In **D. M. Johnson** and **C. E. Erneling** (eds.), *Reassessing the Cognitive Revolution: Alternative Futures*. New York: Oxford University Press.

Cook, D. 1993. Behaviorism evolves. *Educational Technology*, October, 62–77.

Cooper, P. 1993. Paradigm shifts in designed instruction: from behaviorism to cognitivism to constructivism. *Educational Technology*, May, 12–19.

Costall, A. and I. Leuder. 2004. Where is the 'theory' in the theory of mind? *Theory & Psychology*, **14** (5), 623–46.

Crook, C. 1998. Children as computer users: the case of collaborative learning. *Computer and Education*, **30** (3), 237–47.

Cuban, L. 1986. *Teachers and Machines: The Classroom Use of Technology Since 1920*. New York: Teachers College Press.

　2001. *Oversold and Underused: Computers in the Classroom*. Cambridge, MA: Harvard University Press.

Danziger, K. 1985. The methodological imperative in psychology. *Philosophy of the Social Sciences*, **15**, 1–13.

Darwin, C. 1877/1974. A biographical sketch of an infant. In H. Gruber, *Darwin on Man: A Psychological Study of Scientific Creativity*. London: Wildwood House.

De Boysson-Bardies, B., Vihman, M., Roug-Hellichius, L., Durand, C., Landberg, I., and F. Arao, 1993. Material evidence of infant selection from target language: a cross-linguistic study. In C. A. Ferguson, L. Menn, and C. Stoel-Gammon (eds.), *Phonological Development: Models, Research, Implications*. Parkton, MD: York Press.

De Corte, E. 1990. Learning with new information technologies in schools: perspectives from the psychology of learning and instruction. *Journal of Computer Assisted Learning*, **6** (2), 69–87.

Dewey, J. 1916/1966. *Democracy and Education*. New York: Free Press.

　1990. *The School and Society: The Child and the Curriculum*. Chicago: Chicago University Press.

Dilthey, W. 1914–36/1985. *Introduction to the Human Sciences: Wilhelm Dilthey. Selected Works. Vol. 1.* Trans. R. A. Makkreel and F. Rodi, Princeton, NJ: Princeton University Press.

Doherty, M. 2008. *Theory of Mind: How Children Understand Others' Thoughts and Feelings*. Howe, NY: Psychology Press.

Donald, M. 1991. *Origins of the Modern Mind*. Cambridge, MA: Harvard University Press.

Donaldson, M. 1978. *Children's Minds*. London: Fontana.

Durkheim, E. 1922/1956. *Education and Sociology*. Trans. Sherwood D. Fox. Glencoe, IL: Free Press.

Eimas, P. D. 1985. The perception of speech in early infancy. *Scientific American*, January, 46–52.

Elman, J., Bates, E., Johnson, M., Karmiloff-Smith, A., Parisi, D., and K. Plunkett. 1996. *Rethinking Innateness: A Connectionist Perspective on Development.* Cambridge, MA: MIT Press.

Erneling, C. E. 1993. *Understanding Language Acquisition: The Framework of Learning.* Albany, NY: SUNY Press.

1997. Afterword. In **D. M. Johnson** and **C. E. Ernling** (eds.), *The Future of the Cognitive Revolution.* New York: Oxford University Press.

2007. The primacy of social interaction. *American Journal of Psychology,* **120** (2), 334–8.

in press. The limits of mindreading. *Philosophy of the Social Sciences.*

Erneling, C. E. and D. M. Johnson (eds.). 2005. *The Mind as a Scientific Object: Between Brain and Culture.* New York: Oxford University Press.

Evans, C. 1979. *The Mighty Micro: The Impact of the Computer Revolution.* London: Victor Gollancz.

Fodor, J. 1975/1979. *The Language of Thought.* Cambridge, MA: Harvard University Press.

1980. Methodological solipsism considered as a research strategy in cognitive psychology. *Behavioral and Brain Sciences,* **3**, 63–109.

1983. *The Modularity of Mind.* Cambridge, MA: MIT Press.

1987. *Psychosemantics.* Cambridge, MA: MIT Press.

Fuller, S. 2003. *Popper vs. Kuhn: The Struggle for the Soul of Science.* London: Icon Books.

Gardner, H. 1983. *Frames of Mind: The Theory of Multiple Intelligences.* New York: Basic Books.

1985. *The Mind's New Science.* New York: Basic Books.

2004. What we do and don't know about learning. *Daedalus,* Winter, 5–12.

Geary, D. C. 1995. Reflections on evolution and culture in children's cognition: implications for mathematical development and instruction. *American Psychologist,* **50** (1), 24–37.

Gellner, E. 1985. *Relativism and the Social Sciences.* Cambridge: Cambridge University Press.

Gervain, J. and J. Werker. 2008. How infant speech perception contributes to language acquisition. *Language and Linguistics Compass,* **2** (6), 1149–70.

Goffman, E. 1974. *Frame Analysis.* Cambridge, MA: Harvard University Press.

Goodman, N. 1972. *Problems and Projects.* Indianapolis: Bobbs-Merrill.

Gopnik, A. 2004. Finding our inner scientist. *Daedalus,* Winter, 21–8.

2009. *The Philosophical Baby: What Children's Minds Tell Us About Truth, Love, and the Meaning of Life.* New York: Farrar, Straus, and Giroux.

Gopnik, A. and A. N. Meltzoff. 1997. *Words, Thoughts, and Theories*. Cambridge, MA: MIT Press.

Gopnik, A., Meltzoff, A. N., and P. Kuhl, 1999. *The Scientist in the Crib: Minds, Brains, and How Children Learn*. New York: William Morrow.

Gray, H. 1978. Learning to take an object from the mother. In A. Lock (ed.), *Action, Gesture, and Symbol: The Emergence of Language*. New York: Academic Press.

Greenspan, S. and S. Shanker. 2004. *The First Idea: How Symbols, Language, and Intelligence Evolved From Our Early Primate Ancestors to Modern Humans*. Cambridge, MA: Da Capo Press.

Hacking, I. 2002. *Historical Ontology*. Cambridge, MA: Harvard University Press.

Hamlyn, D. W. 1978. *Experience and the Growth of Understanding*. London: Routledge & Kegan Paul.

Harré, R. 1997. 'Berkeleyan' arguments and the ontology of cognitive science. In D. M. Johnson and C. E. Erneling (eds.), *The Future of the Cognitive Revolution*. New York: Oxford University Press.

2000. The rediscovery of the human mind. http://www.massey.ac.nz/xxxAlock/virtual/korea%206/26/00.

2001. Norms in life: problems in the representation of rules. In D. Bakhurst and S. Shanker (eds.), *Jerome Bruner: Language, Culture, Self*. London: Sage.

2002. *Cognitive Psychology: A Philosophical Introduction*. London: Sage.

Harré, R. and G. Gillett. 1994. *The Discursive Mind*. London: Sage.

Harré, R. and F. M. Moghaddam (eds.). 2003. *The Self and Others: Positioning Individuals and Groups in Personal, Political and Cultural Contexts*. Westport, CT: Praeger.

Harré, R. and P. Stearns (eds.). 1995. *Discursive Psychology in Practice*. London: Sage.

Harré, R. and L. van Langehove (eds.). 1999. *Positioning Theory*. Oxford: Blackwell.

Hauser, M. 2000. *Wild Minds: What Animals Really Think*. New York: Henry Holt.

Hazzan, O. 1999. Information technologies and objects to learn with. *Educational Technology*, May–June, 55–9.

Hergenhan, B. R. and M. H. Olson. 1997. *An Introduction to Theories of Learning*. Englewood Cliffs, NJ: Prentice Hall.

Hill, M. 1992. The new literacy beyond the three R's. *Electronic Learning*, September, 28–34.

Hoff-Ginsberg, E. 1997. *Language Development*. Pacific Grove, CA: Brooks/Cole.

Hudspeth, D. 1992. Just-in-time education. *Educational Technology*, June, 7–11.

Hurford, J. R. 2007. *The Origins of Meaning: Language in the Light of Evolution*. New York: Oxford University Press.

Hutto, D. D. 2008. *Folk Psychological Narratives: The Sociocultural Basis of Understanding Reasons*. Cambridge, MA: MIT Press.

Jarvie, I. C. 2005. Workshop rationality, dogmatism, and models of mind. In **C. E. Erneling** and **D. M. Johnson** (eds.), *The Mind as a Scientific Object: Between Brain and Culture*. New York: Oxford University Press.

Johnson, D. M. and **C. E. Erneling** (eds.). 1997. *The Future of the Cognitive Revolution*. New York: Oxford University Press.

Johnson, J. K. 1992. Advancing by the degrees: trends in master's and doctoral programs in educational communication technology. *Tech Trends*, **37** (2), 13–16.

Jonassen, D. H. (ed.). 1996. *Handbook of Research for Educational Communications and Technology*. Mahwah, NJ: Lawrence Erlbaum.

Jonassen, D. H., Carr, C., and **H-P. Yueh**. 1998. Computers as mindtools for engaging learners in critical thinking. *Tech Trends*, March, 24–32.

Juszcyk, P. W. and **C. Derrah.** 1987. Representation of speech sounds by young infants. *Developmental Psychology*, **23**, 648–54.

Juszcyk, P. W., Friederici, A. D., Wessels, J. M., Svenkerud, V. Y., and **A. M. Juszcyk.** 1993. Infants' sensitivity to the sound pattern of native language words. *Journal of Memory and Language*, **32**, 402–20.

Kafai, Y. 1995. *Minds in Play: Computer Game Design as a Context for Children's Learning*. Hillsdale, NJ: Lawrence Erlbaum.

Kagan, J. 1998. *Three Seductive Ideas*. Cambridge, MA: Harvard University Press.

Kearsky, G. 1998. Educational technology: a critique. *Educational Technology*, March–April, 47–51.

Kimbrough Oller, D. 2000. *The Emergence of Speech Capacity*. Mahwah, NJ: Lawrence Erlbaum.

Konner, M. J. 1972. Aspects of the developmental ethology of a foraging people. In **N. J. Blurton Jones** (ed.). *Ethological Studies of Child Behavior*. Cambridge: Cambridge University Press.

Kuhl, P. K. 2004. Early language acquisition: cracking the code. *Nature Reviews Neuroscience*, **5** (11), 831–43.

Kuhn, T. S. 1962. *The Structure of Scientific Revolutions*. Chicago: University of Chicago Press.

Leggett, W. P. and **K. A. Persichitte.** 1998. Blood, sweat and TEARS: 50 years of technology implementation obstacles. *Tech Trends*, April, 33–6.

Leudar, I. and **A. Costall.** 2004. On persistence of the 'problem of "other minds"' in psychology: Chomsky, Grice and theory of mind. *Theory & Psychology*, **14** (5), 601–22.

Leudar, I., Costall, A., and **D. Francis.** 2004. Theory of mind: a critical assessment. *Theory & Psychology,* **14** (5), 571–8.

Lieberman, P. 1984. *The Biology and Evolution of Language.* Cambridge, MA: Harvard University Press.

1985. On the evolution of human syntactic ability: its preadaptive bases – motor control and speech. *Journal of Human Evolution,* **14,** 657–68.

Lieberman, P. and **S. E. Blumstein.** 1988. *Speech Physiology, Speech Perception, and Acoustic Phonetics.* Cambridge: Cambridge University Press.

Linard, M. 1995. New debates on learning support. *Journal of Computer Assisted Learning,* **11** (4) 239–53.

Lock, A. (ed.). 1978. *Action, Gesture, and Symbol: The Emergence of Language.* New York: Academic Press.

Macnamara, J. 1976. Stomachs assimilate and accommodate, don't they? *Canadian Psychological Review,* **17,** 167–73.

MacNeilage, P. F. 2008. *The Origin of Speech.* New York: Oxford University Press.

Malle, B. F. 2004. *How the Mind Explains Behavior: Folk Explanations, Meaning, and Social Interaction.* Cambridge, MA: MIT Press.

Malle, B. F. and **S. Hodges.** 2005. *Other Minds: How Humans Bridge the Divide Between Self and Others.* New York: Guilford Press.

Mandelbaum, M. 1971. *History, Man, and Reason: A Study in Nineteenth-Century Thought.* Baltimore, MD: Johns Hopkins University Press.

Mayer, R. E., Schustack, M. W., and **W. E. Blanton.** 1999. What do children learn from using computers in an informal, collaborative setting? *Educational Technology,* **39,** 27–31.

McCown, R. R. 1999. *Educational Psychology: A Learning-Centred Approach to Classroom Practice.* Scarborough, ONT: Allyn and Bacon.

McGrath, B. 1998. Partners in learning: twelve ways technology changes the teacher–student relationship. *THE Journal,* **25,** 58–61.

McLellan, H. 1994. Situated learning: continuing the conversation. *Educational Technology,* October, 7–8.

Meltzoff, A. N. and **Prinz, W.** (eds.). 2002. *The Imitative Mind.* Cambridge: Cambridge University Press.

Menn, L. and **C. Stoel-Gammon.** 1993. Phonological development: learning sounds and sound patterns. In **J. B. Gleason** (ed.), *The Development of Language.* New York: Macmillan.

Merrill, P., Hammons, K., Tolman, M., Cristensen, L., Vincent, B., and **P. Reynolds.** 1992. *Computers in Education.* Boston: Allyn and Bacon.

Messerly, J. G. 1996. *Piaget's Conception of Evolution: Beyond Darwin and Lamarck.* Lanham, MD: Rowman and Littlefield.

Moghaddam, F. M. 2002. *The Individual and Society: A Cultural Integration.* New York: Worth.

Morss, J. R. 1990. *The Biologising of Childhood: Developmental Psychology and the Darwinian Myth.* Hillsdale, NJ: Lawrence Erlbaum.

Munz, P. 2004. *Beyond Wittgenstein's Poker: New Light on Wittgenstein and Popper.* Burlington, VT: Ashgate

Nagel, T. 1995. *Other Minds: Critical Essays 1969–1994.* New York: Oxford University Press.

Neisser, U. 1988. Five kinds of self-knowledge. *Philosophical Psychology,* **1** (1), 35–59.

Nelson, G. 1998. Internet/web-based instruction and multiple intelligence. *Educational Media International,* **35** (2), 90–4.

Newson, J. 1978. Dialogue and development. In **A. Lock** (ed.), *Action, Gesture, and Symbol: The Emergence of Language.* New York: Academic Press.

Olson, D. R. 1994. *The World on Paper.* Cambridge: Cambridge University Press.

2003. *Psychological Theory and Educational Reform.* Cambridge: Cambridge University Press.

Palermo, D. S. 1971. Is a scientific revolution taking place in psychology? *Science Studies,* **1**, 135–55.

Papert, S. 1980/1993. *Mindstorms: Children, Computers, and Powerful Ideas.* New York: Basic Books.

1993. *The Children's Machine: Rethinking School in the Age of the Computer.* New York: Basic Books.

Piaget, J. 1926/1955. *The Language and Thought of the Child.* New York: Meridian Books.

1928/1976. *Judgement and Reasoning in the Child.* London: Routledge & Kegan Paul.

1936/1963. *The Origins of Intelligence in Children.* New York: International Universities Press.

1937/1954. *The Construction of Reality in the Child.* New York: Basic Books.

1945/1962. *Play, Dreams, and Imagination in Childhood.* New York: Norton.

1947/1976. *The Psychology of Intelligence.* Totowa, NJ: Littlefield.

1948/1973. *To Understand is to Invent: The Future of Education.* New York: Grossman.

1950/1965/1995. *Sociological Studies.* London: Routledge & Kegan Paul.

1964/1968. *Six Psychological Studies.* New York: Vintage Books.

1964/1993. Development and learning. In **M. Gauvin** and **M. Cole** (eds.), *Readings in the Development of Children.* New York: Freeman.

1967/1971. *Biology and Knowledge.* Edinburgh: Edinburgh University Press.

1969/1970. *The Science of Education and the Psychology of the Child*. New York: Grossman.

1970. *Genetic Epistemology*. New York: Columbia University Press.

1970/1971. *Psychology and Genetic Epistemology*. New York: Viking.

1977/1978. *The Development of Thought*. New York: Viking.

1980. The psychogenesis of knowledge and its epistemological significance. In **M. Piattelli-Palmarini** (ed.), *Language and Learning: The Debate Between Jean Piaget and Noam Chomsky*. Cambridge, MA: Harvard University Press.

Piaget, J. and **E. W. Beth**. 1961/1966. *Mathematical Epistemology and Psychology*. Dordrecht: Reidel.

Piattelli-Palmarini, M. (ed.). 1980. *Language and Learning: The Debate Between Jean Piaget and Noam Chomsky*. Cambridge, MA: Harvard University Press.

Pinker, S. 1984. *Language Learnability and Language Development*. Cambridge, MA: Harvard University Press.

1997. *How the Mind Works*. New York: Norton.

2002. *The Blank Slate: The Modern Denial of Human Nature*. New York: Viking.

2007. *The Stuff of Thought: Language as a Window into Human Nature*. New York: Viking.

Plato. 1974. *The Republic*. Trans. **G. M. A. Grube.** Indianapolis: Hackett.

1981. *Plato: Five Dialogues*. Trans. **G. M. A. Grube**. Indianapolis: Hackett.

Popper, K. 1957. *The Poverty of Historicism*. London: Routledge & Kegan Paul.

1963. Back to the Pre-Socratics. In *Conjectures and Refutations: The Growth of Scientific Knowledge*. London: Routledge & Kegan Paul.

1972. *Objective Knowledge: An Evolutionary Approach*. Oxford: Clarendon Press.

Postman, N. 1996. *The End of Education: Redefining the Value of School*. New York: Vintage Books.

1999. *Building a Bridge to the Eighteenth Century*. New York: Alfred A. Knopf.

Premack, D. 1976. *Intelligence in Ape and Man*. Hillsdale, NJ: Lawrence Erlbaum.

Prensky, M. 2001. *Digital Game-Based Learning*. New York: McGraw-Hill.

Putnam, H. 1981. *Reason, Truth, and History*. New York: Cambridge University Press.

Reddy, V. and **P. Morris.** 2004. Participants don't need theories: knowing minds in engagement. *Theory & Psychology*, **14** (5), 647–66.

Relan, A. and **B. B. Gillini**. 1997. Web-based instruction and the traditional classroom: similarities and differences. In **B. H. Khan** (ed.), *Web-Based Instruction*. Englewood Cliffs, NJ: Educational Technologies.

Rich Harris, J. 1998. *The Nurture Assumption: Why Children Turn Out the Way They Do*. New York: Free Press.

Richards, M. (ed.). 1974. *The Integration of a Child into a Social World*. Cambridge: Cambridge University Press.

Rizzolatti, R., Fogassi, L., and **V. Gallese.** 2001. Neurophysiological mechanisms underlying understanding and imitation of action. *Nature Reviews Neuroscience,* **2,** 661–70.

Robinson, D. 1998. *The New Renaissance: Computers and the Next Level of Civilization*. New York: Oxford University Press.

Rogoff, B. 1990. *Apprenticeship in Thinking*. Oxford: Oxford University Press.

   2003. *The Culture of Human Development*. New York: Oxford University Press.

Romiszowski, A. J. 1997. Web-based distance learning and teaching: revolutionary innovation or reaction to necessity. In **B. H. Khan** (ed.), *Web-Based Instruction*. Englewood Cliffs, NJ: Educational Technologies.

Rose, E. 1998. Taking Turing: how the imitation game plays out in the classroom. *Educational Technology,* May–June, 56–61.

   1999. Deconstructing interactivity in educational computing. *Educational Technology,* January–February, 43–9.

Roszak, T. 1986. *The Cult of Information: The Folklore of Computers and the True Art of Thinking*. New York: Pantheon.

Rotman, B. 1977. *Jean Piaget: Psychologist of the Real*. Hassocks: Harvester Press.

Russell, J. 1978. *The Acquisition of Knowledge*. London: Macmillan.

Ryan, J. 1974. Early language development: towards a communicational analysis. In **M. Richards** (ed.), *The Integration of a Child into a Social World*. Cambridge: Cambridge University Press.

Ryle, G. 1949. *The Concept of Mind*. London: Hutchinson.

   1967. Teaching and training. In **R. S. Peters** (ed.), *The Concept of Education*. London: Routledge & Kegan Paul.

Sachs, J. 1993. The emergence of intentional communication. In **J. B. Gleason** (ed.), *The Development of Language*. New York: Macmillan.

Schank, R. C. and **C. Cleary.** 1995. *Engines for Education*. Hillsdale, NJ: Lawrence Erlbaum.

Schoenfeld, W. 1993. The necessity of 'behaviorism'. *Educational Technology,* October, 5–7.

Scott Gordon, H. 1991. *The History and Philosophy of the Social Sciences*. New York: Routledge & Kegan Paul.

Searle, J. 1983. *Intentionality: An Essay in the Philosophy of Mind*. Cambridge: Cambridge University Press.

Shanker, S. 2004. The roots of mindblindness. *Theory & Psychology,* **14** (5), 685–703.

Shanker, S. and T. Taylor. 2005. The significance of ape language research. In C. E. Erneling and D. M. Johnson (eds.), *The Mind as a Scientific Object: Between Brain and Culture*. New York: Oxford University Press.

Sharrock, W. and J. Coulter. 2004. ToM: a critical commentary. *Theory & Psychology*, **14** (5), 579–600.

Shotter, J. 1974. The development of personal powers. In M. Richards (ed.), *The Integration of a Child into a Social World*. Cambridge: Cambridge University Press.

1976. Acquired powers: the transformation of the natural into social powers. In R. Harré (ed.), *Personality*. Totowa, NJ: Rowman and Littlefield.

Shute, V. J. and L. A. Gawlick-Grendell. 1994. What does the computer contribute to learning? *Computers in Education*, **23** (3), 177–86.

Sinclair, H. 1971. Sensorimotor action pattern as a condition for the acquisition of syntax. In E. Ingram and R. Huxley (eds.), *Language Acquisition: Models and Methods*. New York: Academic Press.

Sinnott, J. M., Pison, D. P., and R. N. Askin. 1983. A comparison of pure auditory thresholds in human infants and adults. *Infant Behavior and Development*, 6, 3–18.

Skinner, B. F. 1974. *About Behaviorism*. New York: Random House.

Sykes, W. and R. Reid. 1999. Virtual reality in schools: the ultimate educational technology. *THE Journal*, **26**, 61–3.

Tomasello, M. 1999. *The Cultural Origins of Human Cognition*. Cambridge, MA: Harvard University Press.

2000. Culture and cognitive development. *Current Directions in Psychological Science*, **9**, 37–40.

2008. *Origins of Human Communication*. Cambridge, MA: MIT Press.

Toulmin, S. 1961. *Foresight and Understanding: An Enquiry into the Aims of Science*. New York: Harper and Row.

Van Gelder, T. 2005. Beyond the mind–body problem. In C. E. Erneling and D. M. Johnson (eds.), *The Mind as a Scientific Object: Between Brain and Culture*. New York: Oxford University Press.

Vargas, E. 1993. From behaviorism to selectionism. *Educational Technology*, October, 46–51.

Vasta, R., Haith, M., and S. Miller. 1999. *Child Psychology: The Modern Science*. Second edition. New York: John Wiley & Sons.

Veenema, S. and H. Gardner. 1996. Multimedia and multiple intelligences. *American Prospect*, **27**, 69–75.

Vygotsky, L. 1934/1994. *Thought and Language*. Rev. and ed. A. Kozulin. Cambridge, MA: MIT Press.

1978. *Mind in Society: The Development of Higher Psychological Processes.* Eds. **M. Cole, V. John-Steiner, S. Scriber,** and **E. Souberman.** Cambridge, MA: Harvard University Press.

Walker, S. 1987. The evolution and dissolution of language. In **A. W. Ellis** (ed.), *Progress in Psychology of Language. Vol. 3.* Hillsdale, NJ: Lawrence Erlbaum.

Wallace, P. 1999. *The Psychology of the Internet.* New York: Cambridge University Press.

Wanner, E. and **L. R. Gleitman.** 1982. *Language Acquisition: The State of the Art.* New York: Cambridge University Press.

Wells, G. 1999. *Dialogic Inquiry: Towards a Sociocultural Practice and Theory of Education.* New York: Cambridge University Press.

Werker, J. F., and **R. C. Tees.** 1984. Cross-linguistic speech perception: evidence for perceptual reorganization during the first year of life. *Infant Behavior and Development, 7,* 49–64.

Westera, W. 1999. Paradoxes in open, networked learning environments: towards a paradigm shift. *Educational Technology,* January–February, 17–23.

Wexler, B. E. 2006. *Brain and Culture: Neurobiology, Ideology, and Social Change.* Cambridge, MA: MIT Press.

Williams, E. 2004. Who really needs a 'theory of mind'? An interpretative phenomenological analysis of the autobiographical writings of ten high-functioning individuals with an autism spectrum disorder. *Theory & Psychology,* **14** (5), 704–24.

Winn, W. 1993. Instructional design and situated learning: paradox or partnership? *Educational Technology,* March, 16–21.

Winn, W. and **R. Jackson.** 1999. Fourteen propositions about educational uses of virtual reality. *Educational Technology,* July–August, 5–14.

Wittgenstein, L. 1953. *Philosophical Investigations.* Oxford: Blackwell.

1961. *Tractatus Logico-Philosophicus.* New York: Humanities Press.

Wundt, W. 1916. *Elements of Folk Psychology: Outlines of a Psychological History of the Development of Mankind.* London: Allen & Unwin.

Yarusso, L. 1992. Constructivism vs. objectivism. *Performance & Instruction,* April, 7–9.

Index